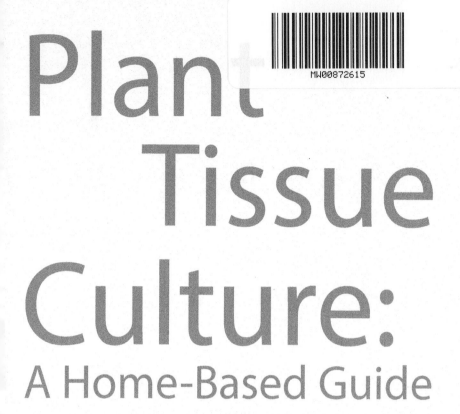

Plant Tissue Culture:
A Home-Based Guide

How to Practice Plant Tissue Culture on a Budget

by Edward Johnson

Acknowledgements

To my caring, loving, and supportive wife, Prarthana. My deepest gratitude to you and the kids. Your encouragement and support are much appreciated. Thanks for putting up with the thousands of plants, piles of potting soil, and dozens of tanks and aquariums.

I'd like to thank all the other plant hobbyists, collectors, and jungle explorers that keep the hobby pulsing along. Keep it up.

Why I Learned to do Plant Tissue Culture at Home

Biotope One started to conserve endemic plants and quickly grew to perform additional functions such as exploring fertilization techniques, plant tissue culture, propagation practices, animal husbandry, and other similar facets and issues enthusiasts encounter. As a result of this exploration for more in-depth information the Biotope Data Collection program was developed to learn more about habitat that these species come from.

Importance is placed on propagation and breeding programs to help curb wild collected species. Locally grown and raised specimens can help reduce the mortality rate of wild collected or poorly cared for species. Collecting data from habitat helps us better understand care requirements to provide better care.

Made up of a loose network of hobby growers, breeders, and hobbyists we work together in common interest keeping species diversity alive and available. Plant and animal keepers form a network to further flora and fauna in the hobby.

www.BiotopeOne.com

Table of Contents

Preface

Cryptocoryne was the first plant I tissue cultured. Bucephalandra and cryptocoryne are some of my favorite aroids for the aquarium and terrarium. I learned how to grow many aquarium plants emersed, or above water, so I had a steady supply for my experiments and displays.

I knew these plants came from jungles halfway around the world but I didn't understand how much of their habitat was being lost.

Chatting with someone that explores the jungle in Malaysia I became aware of a cryptocoryne habitat that had been completely destroyed. In one years time, a small place that once held a particularly nice stand of cryptocoryne had been bulldozed clean.

Timber harvesting, development, and palm oil plantations are having a huge impact on endemic plants. Some of the plants I was interested in only lived in a place the size of a house and nowhere else on earth. They were, and are, being razed so we can have cheap and creamy ice cream.

I started to propagate these plants as much as I could with conventional techniques. One day I ran across plant tissue culture protocols and so my journey began.

It was a sterile environment with expensive gear that was cost prohibitive to me. It seemed like an eternity of researching about how to make do with household items. I started making notes on easy ways to do things which later turned into this book.

I wanted to create a way anyone that could bake a cake could propagate plants with tissue culture at home. I've tried to explain everything as simply as possible.

I encourage everyone to propagate and share plants. Out of this, the Biotope One Plant Library Initiative also began. I wanted to help enthusiasts grow plants, share them, and keep them in cultivation even though they may no longer live in the wilds we let be destroyed.

Here are some cryptocorynes being grown emersed. Often sold as submerged aquarium plants they are contaminated greatly with bacteria from the aquarium. Growing them outside of the aquarium they grow faster and cleaner for explant material for initiation stage. Photo by Edward Johnson

Introduction

Plant tissue culture makes it possible to grow thousands of plants a month in a small room. Start practicing plant tissue culture at the hobby level with tremendous success. Tens of thousands of dollars of equipment isn't needed to start. All that's needed are some readily available items and materials. Everything you need can be found at your local stores or easily ordered online.

Exponential plant growth is possible using plant tissue culture as a means to propagate plants. Just one jar can have the potential to produce 10 or more shoots. Each of these can be split up exponentially. All of those 10 shoots can go into a new jar all by themselves. In a month or two, there can be 100 shoots. In one or two more months those 100 shoots can turn into 1000, 10,000, then 100,000 if you so wish.

Some plants that are tissue cultured with excellent success are aquarium plants, carnivorous plants, and many terrestrial ornamental plants. Begonias, ferns, and even vegetables are readily tissue cultured and produced in huge quantities with minimal effort. An easy and favorite tissue culture plant among beginners and seasoned practitioners is the aquarium plant cryptocoryne.

Many say or hear plant tissue culture cannot be practiced without a huge monetary investment and a large amount of knowledge. This could not be further from the truth. With only a couple hundred dollars one can get started comfortably. It can be done for less if you have some of the materials already or are thrifty.

Many tissue culture suppliers will now sell hobby level practitioners supplies and materials without a special business license. It is also not necessary to order 10,000 pieces of a product as plant tissue culture supply businesses will now sell in smaller minimum orders to

Media inside the vessels contain the nutrients needed to promote plant growth. Plant growth regulators influence cells to create more shoots, grow roots, or elongate shoots. Photo by Edward Johnson

supply hobby level enthusiasts. Buying in larger quantities will often result in better prices per piece. Weigh the cost against its usefulness. Be economically minded and buy what is needed but don't overlook the opportunity for better pricing.

Plant tissue culture can help spread plants to other hobbyists and offer hard to find plants into hobbyists collections. In Borneo, Indonesia, and across the world plant hunters are collecting wild plants before they are decimated by palm oil plantations. This is not a sustainable practice. Tissue culturing these disappearing plants can help keep them alive in the hobby even though they are quickly being lost to deforestation.

Jungles and forests will continue to lose plants because of habitat destruction and over-collecting. Countless endemic plants and undescribed plants have already been lost to just these two practices. There are continual reports of habitat that once held endemic plants, plants that grow nowhere else on earth, being destroyed and lost forever. Why not continue them in cultivation?

To combat these non-sustainable practices and mismanagement of habitat learn to propagate as many of these plants as possible. Many plants that cost $30, $50, or even $100 can be propagated with tissue culture. Make numerous cultures and produce thousands of these plants. Wild collected plants aren't as numerous and cannot fill demand but tissue culturing them can.

More people are likely to buy domestically produced plant tissue cultured plants instead of wild-collected. Healthy plants available locally can be shipped quickly and at a lower cost to the hobbyist. One wild-collected plant that sold for 30 dollars (plus huge import costs) could be offered for 5 dollars and thousands could be made available in a short amount of time.

Plants lost because of habitat destruction that have been collected for the hobby are often still available to enthusiasts. Unfortunately, this does nothing for a wild habitat once these endemic plants are lost. Proceeds from this booklet will go toward projects for helping habitat and species.

An unintended benefit of plant tissue culture was discovered while founding the Biotope One Plant Library. Plant tissue culture made keeping and storing plant species in a very small space a real possibility. Tissue Cultured plants can be manipulated by storing them in a sort of suspended animation. Lower light and cooler temperatures can prolong safe plant storage. This is a great way to keep jars of plants for springtime when they are in higher demand or when shipping is safer because of cold in winter.

Plant tissue culture is an excellent way to propagate tens of thousands of plants for your collection or trading and selling throughout the hobby. Trading excess plants to buy new plant species, tissue culture materials, or new supplies allows profitable growth in the hobby. In a short amount of time make enough money to purchase warehouse racks, lighting, better equipment, and still have excess money.

There are many benefits to learning plant tissue culture. Monetary components that can create income are not the only benefits. Cultures can be shared and shipped easily. Building a plant collection can be greatly augmented with vessels of plantlets. Plants can be stored and maintained longer and in smaller spaces if need be. Money doesn't have to be a motivator to learn. Anyone who enjoys plants for any reason can benefit from the joys of home-based plant tissue culture.

What is Plant Tissue Culture?

Plant tissue culture is the practice of propagating plants in a sterile environment. Plant material is collected that is suitable for initiation and then sterilized. This plant material is known as an explant. Next, the explant is put into a sterile jar of media with nutrients and plant growth regulators which helps it become acclimated to the culture vessel conditions.

Once the plant has become accustomed to the new environment it is multiplied by placing it into a new culture media. At this stage, it can be multiplied further, taken out, or rooted and grown out. In one or two months one cutting can create thousands of plants.

Plants can be artificially manipulated in several ways using plant growth regulators. Plant growth regulators, or PGRs, manipulate plants to multiply, root, and or grow by influencing cell development. Plant growth regulators can also make plants grow multiple new plantlets in a very short amount of time, grow roots, or make the shoots longer.

Meristem material, found at the tip of a stem, can be used to grow many new plantlets quickly. Leaves from plants like Begonia can very quickly produce a large bundle of shoots. Large amounts of genetic clones of the mother plant can quickly be produced. Occasionally a new color or cultivar can be produced but it is not common. Seeds can also be used for plant tissue cultures but do not always produce the exact genetic clones.

Explants must be sterile before putting them into the growth media. Media must be sterile just as explant material must be. Work practices have to produce a sterile environment for explants and vessels. This is an absolute must. It may seem like a difficult task but it is relatively easy to accomplish with practice. Mold and fungus will easily outcompete your explant and ruin your culture if it is not sterile.

Plant tissue culture has four basic stages. The first stage and often the most difficult is initiation. The initiation stage is the first stage and acclimates the new explant to plant tissue culture. Exponential growth occurs in the multiplication stage next. Callus and multiplication stages grow new plant material either as shoots and plantlets or in the callus as a mass of undifferentiated cells to later be manipulated into more callus or plantlet shoots. Rooting is encouraged to produce a root system in order to be planted out. Plants are then hardened off so they can acclimate to life outside of the artificial conditions they were grown in.

Plant tissue culture is commonly used in large-scale terrestrial ornamental plant production, carnivorous plants, and aquatic plant production. Some of the largest plant nurseries have their own tissue culture labs. Nurseries often buy large numbers of plantlets from plant tissue culture labs to grow out and these are referred to as liners.

Another commercial practice is to contact a plant tissue culture laboratory and have them manage the process. This involves supplying the plant specimens to culture. A predetermined amount of plants are contracted for production. A plant tissue culture lab would produce a number of plantlets, perhaps 25,000 plants a month for their customer. Upfront fees are common and payment is made when the plants are provided. This can be costly initially because of the scale of production.

This guide will teach you how to begin plant tissue culture at home with minimal investment. You can tailor your setup easily to your own needs and concentrate on one single plant species or a wide variety. Growing hundreds or tens of thousands of plants is a very real possibility.

Media inside the vessels contain the nutrients needed to promote plant growth. Plant growth regulators influence cells to create more shoots, grow roots, or elongate shoots. Photo by Edward Johnson

Safety Procedures

Safety is a very important part of plant tissue culture. Potential safety issues that may be encountered have been brought to your attention when possible. Procedures outlined in this booklet follow generally adopted steps and precautions in the field of plant tissue culture and lab work.

Your work environment and practices dictate your safety as well as those around you. Use caution and common sense. No one else can accept any responsibility for your actions.

Before continuing with plant tissue culture each practitioner should calculate their risk assessment. Errors and omissions can be made and this booklet is no substitute for personal safety or procedure safety.

Use common sense and foresight. Use caution and care when working in a lab environment and with chemicals and tools.

Make sure work is carried out in a suitable environment with adequate ventilation and lighting.

Read owner's manuals and product labels to become familiar with each products operating instructions, safety precautions, warnings, and dangers.

Make sure care is taken while pouring liquids, using heating substances, and storing items that are sharp or otherwise dangerous.

Be aware that alcohol and ethanol are flammable and use precautions to avoid open flame around alcohol and ethanol.

Use protective gear when using chemicals and plant growth regu-

Components recommended for home plant tissue culture can be dangerous. Carelessness and oversight should be avoided at all costs. Wear your protective gear! Be safe! Photo by Edward Johnson

lators such as protective gloves and protective eyewear. Skin contact with some chemicals can be dangerous. Some chemicals can cause permanent eye damage so wear eye protection to avoid getting chemicals into your eyes.

Wear a disposable jumpsuit to avoid chemicals from getting on your clothing or skin. Some chemicals can cause internal organ failure if mishandled.

It is not suggested to use the more dangerous chemicals available for use in plant tissue culture. While more dangerous and potentially deadly chemicals are available for use, the chemicals used in this guide are not without potentially serious health hazards and risks.

Handle, store, and dispose of all materials safely and responsibly.

Content contained in this guide is not meant to replace the safety warnings on product labels nor does it replace the manufacturers' safe handling practices outlined in their product sheets or MSDS sheets. Follow the manufacturers' safety precautions. Manufacturer safety practices supersede any use or instruction contained within this guide.

Supplies and Materials

Lab equipment is expensive. There are many ways to avoid costly gear. Typically, one would use a laminar flow hood, an autoclave, media dispensers, lab-grade meters, scales, and tools. Combined these things alone would place the price of starting up a small tissue culture lab into the tens of thousands of dollars.

Luckily, improvising much of this gear can reduce the cost to a fraction. A laminar flow hood can be replaced with a glass aquarium or plastic storage tote. Pressure cookers can do the same work that autoclaves do in a scientific grade lab or commercial lab.

Scientific papers often use the most expensive plant growth regulators because they are well funded. Often results ranging close to them can be obtained with other plant growth regulators.

Replacing this expensive gear with commonly available supplies and materials can be done with great success.

Workspace for a sterile area to work
Aquarium
Plastic Bin or Tote
Glovebox
Flow-Through Hood

Pressure Cooker for Sterilizing Vessels
Autoclave or Pressure Cooker.
Microwave for sterilizing small batches.

Vessels
Baby Food Jars for cultures.
Small bandaids for covering the hole in the original lid.
Magenta B caps for reusable lids.

Antibacterial Soap
Antibacterial soap is good for cleaning explants in the first step of sterilization.

Measuring Scale
Accurate scale down to milligrams for weighing chemicals.

Measuring Spoons and Cups
"Smidgeon" measuring set for quick measurements.
Graduated container 1 liter or larger to measure liquids.
Paper condiment cups for weighing powders.
Plastic/glass pipettes for measuring small amounts of liquid.
Graduated syringe for filling vessels (30ml minimum).

Small Hand Tools
Forceps to grasp and move explant material into vessels.
Scalpel with plastic handle preferably.
Tweezers for fine work with explants and plantlets.

PH Meter

PH meter is needed to reliably set media pH.

7.0 Testing solution to calibrate the meter.

4.0 Testing solution to calibrate the meter.

Cleaning/storage solution for the meter.

Common General Supplies

Baking Soda for lowering PH of media.

White vinegar for raising the PH of media.

Spray bottles for sterilizing solutions.

Plastic cling wrap to protect vessels from contamination.

Food coloring for tracking media.

Mini refrigerator to store chemicals.

Expensive scientific supplies can often be improvised or found inexpensively. Thriftiness can be an asset. Finding deals or less expensive options will also help pay off in plant tissue culture at home. Photo by Edward Johnson

Cooking Utensils

Pot with a lid to heat media.

Plastic ladle for stirring and dispensing.

Media Supplies

PGRs: BAP, IBA, NAA, Kinetin, 2iP

PPM (Plant Preservative Mixture)

Agar Powder

Inositol

Thiamin

Vitamin C

Murashige and Skoog Media

Tissue Culture Vessels

Plant tissue culture couldn't be practiced without sterile vessels to hold your media and plant material. Luckily, many containers are also easily sterilized and used. Most of them are also reusable many times and can easily be repurposed for plant tissue culture.

Being creative when looking for potential vessels can save a lot of money. Friends and coworkers often will save their glass containers for you if you notice they have a habit of drinking from suitable containers. Certain sizes have benefits in certain stages and paying attention to the best use of materials and space will provide the most return. Use small jars for smaller plants and large jars for bigger species to make the most of the room you have.

Thin test tube vessels make great initiation phase vessels while wide-mouth canning jars make exceptional vessels for multiplying fast-growing bushy plants. Baby food jars are in the middle of the aisle as they offer good space-saving potential while keeping plenty of plantlets safe and happy.

Larger vessels offer the option of allowing plantlets to grow and use up hormone to begin rooting, saving steps. Smaller jars allow for fast-growing multiplication stages to be split and replated quickly to multiply efficiently. Each size has its benefit and setbacks. Using these benefits will create advantages and increase productivity.

Vessels must be made of materials that can withstand the high heat in the autoclave. Glass can most easily withstand these temperatures but not all plastics can. For this reason, polypropylene plastics (PP) are used in the autoclave. Most plastics marked with PP can be autoclaved, with some limits. Thin deli tubs marked PP can be used with enough venting to allow them not to crush when cooling down.

The most trusted and widely used vessels throughout the industry are specially made for plant tissue culture. While they are the most durable and reliable they are also the most costly option. Some vessels easily cost 10 US dollars each. In the long term it will amortize and pay itself off but those wanting or needing to start on a tight budget might opt for a more cost-friendly option.

There are many great commercially available vessels in many configurations. They are largely very durable and will last for an extended time. Some options include square containers for saving space, round ones with screw-on lids, and easy to use slip-on lids for glass containers.

Baby food jars are an excellent vessel to use when trying to save money. The metal lids that come on the jars can be reused by poking a hole in the lid. Small round bandages used for shaving nicks can be placed over the hole to keep it sterile after autoclaving.

Another option is to use a larger hole and use a rectangular piece of sponge shoved into the hole. The sponge method allows the lids to

There are many kinds of vessels available. Test tubes, baby food jars, deli tubs, and other food jars can be used for plant tissue culture. Venting can be done with lids using a nail and a small bandage or sponge cube. Photo by Edward Johnson

be reused several times where the bandage method needs the bandage replaced each time. The benefit of the bandage method is that they are easier to stack.

Magenta makes a lid for use with baby food jars. They offer vented and non vented plastic caps that slip on over the glass baby food jars. Magenta B Cap lids help make the job easier by allowing the cap to be easily put on after plating. Even some smaller commercial labs use baby food jars with Magenta B Cap lids.

Ads placed in local newspapers or online For Sale/Wanted sites are good resources for baby food jars. Thrifty and eco-friendly parents will save baby food jars for reuse and offer them occasionally but the best results come from offering a small amount per useable baby food jar.

Canning jars make also very useful and versatile vessels for plant tissue culture. Canning jar sized lids are available from Magenta that fit the threads of half-pint, pint, and quart jars in both regular and wide-mouth sizes. These jars are easy to gather and the lids can be purchased in lots of 100 for convenience if you need that many at a time. Canning jars can often be found on the for sale and wanted sections in local papers and online sites.

Almost any glass jar can be used as a vessel in plant tissue culture. Single serving cold coffee drink jars with a wide mouth work very well for many plants and are easy to find. Most glass jars will need to have the lid reused several times using the vent methods but will rust eventually. Light rust doesn't seem to affect the sterility of vessels but when it scales it should be replaced. Replacing missing or damaged metal lids with tin foil is an appropriate method but will allow for slightly higher numbers of contaminated vessels as they do not seal as tightly and securely.

Polypropylene plastic deli tubs can be used and are cheap to use. 16-ounce to 32-ounce bins are easy to find. The problem with them is that they are thin and will collapse under the weight of each other when autoclaved if not stacked carefully. They must be evenly placed to disperse the weight of the ones above them by alternating them at a 45-degree angle so that two are below the one on top.

Deli tub lids must be well vented using the sponge or bandage method. If they are not highly vented either the expansion from heating will push the lids off or the contraction from cooling will suck them flat and make them unusable. 2 bandages with a 1/4 inch hole is usually enough ventilation. Test your deli tubs with your method of autoclaving to make sure before processing an entire batch to make sure you have the method working.

32-ounce deli tubs also make an excellent container for taller plants, like bamboo, or fast growers. The extra height allows for longer growing times in vessels so that plantlets can start rooting on their own after they use up the plant hormones in the media. Plantlets can sometimes go straight from multiplication to hardening off, or even moved to the greenhouse while still in-vitro to acclimate while saving steps and ultimately time.

Test tubes made of glass are useful for initiation and small plantlets. Glass test tubes can use a sponge cube to protect the opening from contamination. Polypropylene test tubes made for plant tissue culture are especially handy and are available from most online plant tissue culture suppliers.

Test tubes with screw-on lids make it very easy to use, especially when plating explants. Initiation phases often use only one or two explants per vessel to lower chances of contamination and the small size of test tubes is perfect for making the most out of resources. Media goes a lot further in smaller vessels which means more explants can be initiated with the same amount.

Whatever vessels used must be able to withstand the high heat of an autoclave or pressure cooker. Never put a jar and lid in the autoclave or pressure cooker that is completely sealed. It must be vented with a slightly loose cap or a sterile venting mechanism to avoid accidents. Glass jars should be free of nicks and chips as heating and cooling can easily break a damaged glass jar.

Plant Growth Regulators

Plant cells naturally can create cells for leaves, roots, and other plant parts. Using plant growth regulators those processes can be controlled or induced into action. Plant growth regulators, or PGRs, influence plant cells directly to grow roots, shoots, or callus in cultures. Normally, external conditions might influence these changes.

Cells can be influenced to create new growth in different stages of tissue culture. There are several types of plant growth regulators commonly used for this: auxins, cytokinins, and gibberellins. Each one performs specific useful functions.

Cytokinins are the most important plant growth regulators used in tissue culture. Cytokinins are plant growth regulators that primarily create cell division. It is especially useful for the multiplication stage of tissue culture.

BAP (6-benzyl amino purine) is very common and is useful for creating multiple shoots from one explant. It can be responsible for turning one piece of plant material into a bundle of tiny plantlets. These plantlets can be divided and put into fresh new multiplication media to be further multiplied and divided exponentially.

Cytokinins do little to create root growth in most plants. When rooting in cultures occurs most of the cytokinins have been utilized and metabolized out by the plants. With the now lack of cytokinins, the plant starts to grow roots on its own. It is no longer being artificially influenced to multiply.

Auxins are another popular plant growth regulator. Auxins primarily contribute to better rooting. Auxins limit side shoots and other similar shoot tip growth in favor of developing a root system.

Plant growth regulators need to be weighed carefully. Powders should be put into solutions that are easy to measure on the fly. Typically 1mg/ml is an easy way to make PGR solutions for ease of use. Photo by Edward Johnson

Plants that are hard to get rooted outside of cultures, in wet perlite, for example, could benefit from having Auxins put into the medium either in a multiplication or a dedicated rooting medium. This could save a lot of time in production if it allows rooting in multiplication which would avoid putting the culture into a rooting media or long ex-vitro rooting in the greenhouse.

Gibberellins are worth mentioning here also because GA3 has a place in your tissue culture tool kit. GA3 treatments are useful for seeds to break dormancy in those seeds that need stratifying treatment. Many carnivorous plants need cold stratification and GA3 can induce growth, avoiding months-long cold storage procedures.

GA3 also regulates young shoots where it will control stem elongation by encouraging cell division and elongation. Auxins only stimulate cell elongation. This is why you will occasionally see GA3 in a plant protocol alongside other plant growth regulators.

Auxins

IAA
Indole-3-Acetic Acid
Adventurous Root Formation

IBA
Indole-3-Butyric Acid
Adventurous shoot formation

NAA
A-Napthaleneacetic Acid
Callus Formation and Growth

2,4D
2,4-D Dichlorophenoxyacetic Acid

Inhibition of Axillary Buds

Cytokinins

BAP
6-Benylaminopurine
Adventitious Shoot Formation

2iP
6-y,y-Dimethylallylaminopurine
Promotes Cell Division

Kinetin
6-Furfurylaminopurine
Callus Initiation and Growth

TDZ
Thidiazuron
Axillary Bud Break and Growth

Zeatin
6- (4-hydroxy-3-methylbut-2-enylamino)
Inhibits Leaf Senescence

Gibberellins

GA3
Gibberellic Acid
Shoot elongation. Dormancy.

Regulator	Molecular Weight	Dissolves in	mg/l
ABA	264.3	1N KOH	3.78
BAP	225.3	Alcohol	4.44
2iP	203.2	1N KOH	4.92
2,4D	221.0	1N KOH	4.52
GA3	346.4	1N KOH	2.89
IAA	175.2	Alcohol	5.71
IBA	203.2	Alcohol	4.90
Kinetin	215.2	Alcohol	4.65
NAA	186.2	Alcohol	5.37
TDZ	220.2	1N KOH	4.54
Zeatin	219.2	1N KOH	4.56

Setting Up Your Lab

Home-based laboratories have many options and combinations which can be used to successfully practice plant tissue culture. Dedicated rooms used for tissue culture can nearly be as successful as using the kitchen table. The organization, planning, and patience is key to a successful tissue culture project at home.

Draft free and traffic-free areas will give you the best success. Lots of bacteria and fungus spores drift with air movement. Avoid dust and spores from landing on cultures under the hood. Find a quiet and still area for your workspace and hood. Avoid areas where people might walk back and forth nearby.

Consider also that chemicals will be used, so, avoid areas where this may present a problem. Don't get chemicals on, or use chemicals in, home use items and avoid staining or damaging floors or tables. Make sure your equipment is dedicated to your plant tissue culture and not moved back and forth from the kitchen cupboard or used for eating.

Plastic storage bins and glass aquariums make inexpensive alternatives to laminar flow hoods. Proper procedures and caution can provide a very high rate of success from contamination. Photo by Edward Johnson

Some plant tissue culture supplies can be stored in a freezer or refrigerator to extend their useable life. It is best to have a dedicated mini refrigerator to use only for plant tissue culture. With extreme care and caution, some do use their household refrigerator and freezer.

If using the household refrigerator or freezer make certain everything is marked with extreme care as to what it is. Remember, exposure and contact with some particular chemicals can be hazardous to your health. Read your product MSDS sheets and manufacturer recommendations on handling and storage before use.

A used mini refrigerator freezer is ideal as dedicated cold storage for materials needing refrigeration. Label everything clearly. Powders and concentrated chemicals should be labeled and stored in the freezer section to prolong their shelf life.

A desk or table should be neat and organized to avoid confusion and accidents. Sit directly in front of your hood and at a comfortable working height. Desks should have ample room to allow comfort.

On one side of your workspace place a spray bottle of disinfectant along with a roll of clean paper towels in case of an accident. On the other side place items that will go into the hood. This makes it easy to pick up an item with one hand and spray it with disinfectant using the other as it is placed under the hood. You will then spray your gloved hands and place them under the hood.

Having a workspace neat and orderly will reduce movements and help prevent contamination in jars. Placing your items in the same place every time will breed familiarity and help ensure minimal movements and confusion. Have a trashcan handy near your feet to dispose of used paper towels or gloves quickly, easily, and properly.

Many operations do not need to be performed at your clean hood area. Making media or sterilizing explants can be done in a different location. Of course, all of this can be done in one area if needed. Neatly organizing and storing materials will save a lot of time and prevent accidents.

Always make sure chemicals are clearly labeled and out of reach of children and irresponsible adults. Most of the chemicals used and working with are safe and will not likely cause immediate death or injury. It nonetheless can be very dangerous if handled improperly.

Lighting Racks

Plants use photosynthesis to create energy to live and grow. Media used to grow explants contain all the nutrients plants will need. It is because of this that lower levels of artificial light can be used to grow plants. Plants do not need to fully rely on photosynthesis.

It is not necessary to provide natural levels of light and in some examples, it is detrimental to plant growth and development.

Standard fluorescent tube lighting or LED lighting can be used with more than satisfactory results. Fluorescent lighting is readily available and easy to use in the form of shop lights.

Shop lights come in easy to find standard lengths of 18 inches, 24 inches, and 48 inches. When purchasing or building a rack for plants take these measurements into consideration. Buy a shop light fluorescent fixture to fit the rack. On the underside of each shelf mount your fluorescent shop light. Use the top rack for storage or mount light from the ceiling for an extra level.

When choosing a shelf depth determine what size plastic totes to be used. The best use of space would be a 48-inch wide shelf and 24 inches deep. Placing a single layer of eight plastic bins per shelf would provide space for hundreds or thousands of plantlets, easily.

By placing two 48 inch shop lights above each shelf it is possible to stack two layers of plastic totes and still have excellent results. Every two days to a week check the cultures and rotate the bottom bins to the top of the stack if concerns or issues arise.

There are different colors of lighting available and can be compared somewhat by using the Kelvin rating. Some lighting looks yellow and some will look more blue or white. Lighting with a color temperature of 2300 Kelvin will appear more yellow and a 6500 Kelvin will appear brighter and bluish-white.

The color range is mostly for your personal preference. What is more important to the plant is the lumens or output of light the bulbs give off.

People tend to like a more natural color and a color temperature of 5000K or 5500K will be more friendly to your eyes. The Kelvin or color temperature will be labeled on the package of the bulbs. Anything from 3500 to 6700 Kelvin will work for growing plants.

Most people would prefer 5500 Kelvin as is it is easier on the eyes and makes recognizing contamination relatively easy.

Setting timers on lighting rack systems will save a lot of bothers. A photoperiod of 12 to 16 hours a day is most often used for best results. Generally, 12 hours of light per day is sufficient for the initiation, multiplication, and rooting stages.

Hardening off plants right out of culture or rooting plants will benefit greatly from a 12-hour photoperiod until they have rooted or become acclimated to the ex-vitro conditions.

After plants are taken out of culture, acclimated, and rooted they may need more intense lighting for optimal growth depending on the plant species requirements. Fluorescent tubes available as shop lighting should be more than ample for almost all tissue cultured plants to get them started and on their way out to the greenhouse.

Light racks can be made with shop fluorescent shop lighting. Placing cultures in plastic totes helps reduce contamination from dust and moving air inside your tissue culture room. Photo by Edward Johnson

Popular Protocols

Plant tissue culture has already attracted a list of species that are commonly cultured. Carnivorous plants were probably some of the first ones propagated using plant tissue culture at the hobbyist level.

Venus flytraps, sundews, and most other carnivorous plants use a lower concentration of media such as Murashige and Skoog and plant growth regulators than most other non-carnivorous plants. Some carnivorous plants can even be grown satisfactorily without any plant growth regulators in the media.

There are many plants that already have protocols available. Protocols are basically a recipe and instruction set that has had success. For the most part though, many commercial entities do not and will not share their protocols to protect their time and monetary investment. As a result of this, you'll find that scientific papers are your best source of known protocols.

Scientific papers on plant tissue culture usually go into great detail.

The protocols in most of these journal papers tell us which plant growth regulators were used, what media, and any other ingredients being testing in the protocol. Other details are often included in the abstract such as what plant material they use for the initiating explant.

Often there will not be an entire scientific paper available for free. The abstract in the front, which is more often available free, can give you a huge advantage over starting without any information. Gather as much information as the abstract divulges and layout a plan.

One thing worth mentioning about scientific papers written from university experiments is that they tend to be funded well and have

Protocols are like recipes for mixing your media. Every plant has an optimal protocol that grows and roots the best. There is often a protocol for initiation, multiplication, and rooting. They all can require different components. Photo by Edward Johnson

grants to support them. Therefore, they can use the most expensive chemicals and time-consuming procedures for their protocol. Since we are trying to both propagate plants and save time and money we can often use less expensive chemicals and get satisfactory results.

As an example, a protocol that calls for expensive Zeatin can be tried using less expensive BAP. Zeatin costs a lot more than BAP and is riskier to work with health-wise. Using a substitute may or may not get the same amount of explants but with the extra expense saved it can still end up being productive and cost-effective.

Frequently, there are no protocols or papers published for plants wishing to fo into tissue culture. Looking at protocols of related species can often give a hint about where to start. If there are no closely related protocols to be found consider what next closest plants might have the same properties and start trying with those protocols.

Getting plants that are wild-collected from destroyed jungles ready for palm oil plantations may even be undescribed. They have no scientific name yet. For these plants, there are no protocols available so look for the most closely related plant to find a protocol.

Carefully grow the plants so as not kill them. Take explants and experiment until a protocol works and clean cultures are obtained. Keep notes and adjust my media until the best results are obtained. It is a lot of work but it is rewarding when you get it right.

Homemade Tissue Culture Media Solution

Some plants can be cultured with DIY media. This media will work for some carnivorous plants and easier aquatic plants. MS (Murashige and Skoog) or other pre-made media will give better results. Some carnivorous plants like Venus FLy Trap and some Drosera will multiply without plant growth regulators, albeit more slowly.

DIY Media

1/8 cup table sugar
1 cup water
1/2 cup stock solution (Miracid diluted 1/4 tsp in 1 gallon water)
1/2 inositol tablet (125mg)
1/4 vitamin tablet with thiamin
2 Tablespoons agar flakes

Protocols for Popular Plants

Aponogeten

Explant

Young tuber segments with meristems. Also from the seed of mature plants.

Tuber: Rinse the whole segment in running tap water for 20 minutes. Dip in 91% alcohol. Transfer to 3% Hydrogen Peroxide and shake for 3 to 5 minutes for young explant material or 5 to 7 minutes for older explant material. Transfer to 250 ml of 10% bleach solution with one drop of baby shampoo as a surfactant. Shake for 10 minutes.

Seed: Dip in 91% alcohol. Transfer to 3% Hydrogen Peroxide and shake for 3 to 5 minutes for young explant material or 5 to 7 minutes for older explant material. Transfer to 250 ml of 10% bleach solution with one drop of baby shampoo as a surfactant. Shake for 3 minutes.

Rinse in sterile water twice under your hood. Under the hood with sterile tools cut segment into pieces removing the stem of the plant to avoid sterilant uptake. Seeds can be laid into the surface of the media.

Initiation

1 liter of distilled water
Murashige & Skoog (MS) Basal Salt Mixture
1 mg/ml of BAP
1 mg/ml NAA
1 ml of PPM
5 grams of Agar
30 grams of table sugar or sucrose
2-3 drops of food coloring for easy identification
pH adjusted to 5.6 - 5.8

Many plants will root when the BAP is exhausted so there may be no need to go to the multiplication or rooting stage. Simply divide and replate in new media or harden off.

Multiplication

1 liter of distilled water
Murashige & Skoog (MS) Basal Salt Mixture
1 mg/l of BAP
3 mg/l NAA
1 ml of PPM
5 grams of Agar
30 grams of table sugar or sucrose
2-3 drops of food coloring for easy identification
pH adjusted to 5.6 - 5.8

Plantlets may root when BAP and NAA are exhausted so it can be possible to omit the rooting stage and go straight to hardening off. Otherwise, replate to further multiply.

Rooting

1 liter of distilled water
Murashige & Skoog (MS) Basal Salt Mixture
2 mg/l BAP
1 mg/l NAA
1 ml of PPM
5 grams of Agar
30 grams of table sugar or sucrose
2-3 drops of food coloring for easy identification
pH adjusted to 5.6 - 5.8

Rooting media is devoid of plant growth regulators. As an alternative to rooting media, a plastic shoebox with perlite and water will root divided plantlets in 2 to 3 weeks' time so that rooting stage media may be omitted. After plantlets have rooted in perlite and water they can be hardened off.

Hardening

Divide rooted plantlets into individual plants or small groups. Using a 4:1 ratio of perlite and peat place plantlets in media using either plastic storage bins with a lid or nursery 1020 trays with cells and humidity dome. Humidity at 60 to 80 percent is optimal to start. Gradually open lids to acclimate to room humidity.

Begonia Rex

Explant

Seeds or young clean leaf disc segments 1 cm square as explant material.

Rinse the whole leaf in running tap water for 20 minutes. Dip in 91% alcohol. Transfer to 3% Hydrogen Peroxide and shake for 3 to 5 minutes for young explant material or 5 to 7 minutes for older explant material. Transfer to 250 ml of 10% bleach solution with one drop of baby shampoo as a surfactant. Shake for 10 minutes.

Rinse in sterile water twice under the hood. Still under the hood with sterile tools cut the leaf into 1 cm square pieces removing the stem of the plant to avoid sterilant uptake.

Initiation

1 liter of distilled water
Murashige & Skoog (MS) Basal Salt Mixture
1.0 mg/ml of BAP (omit if using seeds)
.5 mg/ml IBA
1 ml of PPM
5 grams of Agar
30 grams of table sugar or sucrose
2-3 drops of food coloring for easy identification
pH adjusted to 5.6 - 5.8

Plants may root when the BAP is exhausted so there may be no need to go to the multiplication or rooting stage. Divide and replate in new multiplication media or remove from culture and harden off.

Multiplication

1 liter of distilled water
Murashige & Skoog (MS) Basal Salt Mixture
1.0 mg/ml of BAP
.5 mg/ml IBA
.2 mg/ml GA3
1 ml of PPM
5 grams of Agar
30 grams of table sugar or sucrose

2-3 drops of food coloring for easy identification
pH adjusted to 5.6 - 5.8

Plantlets may root when BAP is exhausted so it can be possible to omit the rooting stage and go straight to hardening off.

Rooting

1 liter of distilled water
1/2 strength Murashige & Skoog (MS) Basal Salt Mixture
1 ml of PPM
5 grams of Agar
30 grams of table sugar or sucrose
2-3 drops of food coloring for easy identification
pH adjusted to 5.6 - 5.8

Hardening

Divide rooted plantlets into individual plants or small groups. Using a 4:1 ratio of perlite and peat place plantlets in media using either plastic storage bins with a lid or nursery 1020 trays with cells and humidity dome. Humidity at 60 to 80 percent is optimal to start. Gradually open lids to acclimate to room humidity.

Cryptocoryne and Lagenandra

Explant: Runner tip sterilized with 10 percent bleach.

Initiation

1 liter of distilled water
Murashige & Skoog (MS) Basal Salt Mixture
1 mg/ml of BAP
1 ml of PPM

5 grams of Agar
30 grams of table sugar or lab grade sucrose
2-3 drops of food coloring for easy identification
pH adjusted to 5.6 - 5.8

Multiplication

1 liter of distilled water
Murashige & Skoog (MS) Basal Salt Mixture
5 mg/ml of BAP
1 ml of PPM
5 grams of Agar
30 grams of table sugar or sucrose
2-3 drops of food coloring for easy identification
pH adjusted to 5.6 - 5.8

Rooting

Cryptocoryne and laganendra can be kept in the vessels until they start rooting on their own when the BAP is used up by the plant. If you want to promote plant rootlets use .5 mg/ml of IBA in your multiplication media. Some cryptocorynes respond better to IBA and IAA than other cryptocoryne species.

Hardening

Plantlets can be separated by teasing the root mass apart gently. Place each plant in wet potting soil in a plastic tote or place each plantlet or a small bundle of plantlets into rockwool and place in 1020 nursery trays with a sealed bottom. 72-cell inserts for a non-draining 1020 nursery flat works well for growing nice cryptocoryne and lagenandra on an indoor rack. Do not let the non-draining rack dry out.

Nepenthes

Explant

Seeds or young clean shoot tips as explant material. Cut shoot tip long. Trim shoot tip shorter after sterilization to prevent stem uptake of sterilant through capillary action.

Nepenthes seeds should be very fresh. Seeds are fine and using a tea bag to contain seeds during sterilization is helpful.

Rinse in running tap water for 20 minutes. Dip in 91% alcohol. Transfer to 3% Hydrogen Peroxide and shake for 3 to 5 minutes for young explant material or 5 to 7 minutes for older explant material. Transfer to 250 ml of 10% bleach solution with one drop of baby shampoo as a surfactant. Shake for 5 to 10 minutes. Rinse in sterile water twice under your hood and transfer to your media.

Initiation

1 liter of distilled water
1/2 strength Murashige & Skoog (MS) Basal Salt Mixture
.5 mg/ml of BAP (omit if using seeds)
1 ml of PPM
5 grams of Agar
30 grams of table sugar or sucrose
2-3 drops of food coloring for easy identification
pH adjusted to 5.6 - 5.8

Many plants will root when the BAP is exhausted so there may be no need to go to the multiplication or rooting stage. Simply divide and replate in new media or harden off.

Multiplication

1 liter of distilled water

1/2 strength Murashige & Skoog (MS) Basal Salt Mixture

.5 mg/ml of BAP

1 ml of PPM

5 grams of Agar

30 grams of table sugar or sucrose

2-3 drops of food coloring for easy identification

pH adjusted to 5.6 - 5.8

Plantlets may root when BAP is exhausted so it can be possible to omit the rooting stage and go straight to hardening off.

Rooting

1 liter of distilled water

1/2 strength Murashige & Skoog (MS) Basal Salt Mixture

.1 mg/ml of IBA

1 ml of PPM

5 grams of Agar

30 grams of table sugar or sucrose

2-3 drops of food coloring for easy identification

pH adjusted to 5.6 - 5.8

Hardening

Divide rooted plantlets into individual plants or small groups. Using a 1:1 ratio of peat and coarse sand place plantlets in media using either plastic storage bins with a lid or nursery 1020 trays with cells and humidity dome. Gradually open lids to acclimate to room humidity.

Saintpaulia "African violet"

Explant

Seeds or young clean leaf disc segments 1 cm square as explant material.

Rinse the whole leaf in running tap water for 20 minutes. Dip in 91% alcohol. Transfer to 3% Hydrogen Peroxide and shake for 3 to 5 minutes for young explant material or 5 to 7 minutes for older explant material. Transfer to 250 ml of 10% bleach solution with one drop of baby shampoo as a surfactant. Shake for 10 minutes.

Rinse in sterile water twice under your hood. Still under the hood with sterile tools cut the leaf into 1 cm square pieces. Remove the end of the stem of the leaf to avoid sterilant uptake.

Initiation

1 liter of distilled water
Murashige & Skoog (MS) Basal Salt Mixture
.4 mg/ml of BAP (omit if using seeds)
.1 mg/ml NAA
1 ml of PPM
5 grams of Agar
30 grams of table sugar or sucrose
2-3 drops of food coloring for easy identification
pH adjusted to 5.6 - 5.8

Many plants will root when the BAP is exhausted so there may be no need to go to the multiplication or rooting stage. Simply divide and replate in new media or harden off.

Multiplication

1 liter of distilled water
Murashige & Skoog (MS) Basal Salt Mixture
.4 mg/ml of BAP
.1 mg/ml NAA
1 ml of PPM
5 grams of Agar
30 grams of table sugar or sucrose
2-3 drops of food coloring for easy identification
pH adjusted to 5.6 - 5.8

Plantlets may root when BAP is exhausted so it can be possible to omit the rooting stage and go straight to hardening off.

Rooting

1 liter of distilled water
Murashige & Skoog (MS) Basal Salt Mixture
1 ml of PPM
5 grams of Agar
30 grams of table sugar or sucrose
2-3 drops of food coloring for easy identification
pH adjusted to 5.6 - 5.8

Rooting media is devoid of plant growth regulators. As an alternative to rooting media, a plastic shoebox with perlite and water will root divided plantlets in 2 to 3 weeks' time. The rooting stage in media may be omitted by rooting them this way. After plantlets have rooted in perlite and water they can be hardened off.

Hardening

Divide rooted plantlets into individual plants or small groups. Using a 4:1 ratio of perlite and peat place plantlets in media using either plastic storage bins with a lid or nursery 1020 trays with cells and humidity dome. Humidity at 60 to 80 percent is optimal to start. Gradually open lids to acclimate to room humidity.

Venus Fly Traps

Explant

Seeds or young clean unopened trap, or flower stalk as explant material. Cut stalk or trap stem long. Trim stem/stalk shorter after sterilization to prevent stem uptake of sterilant through capillary action.

Rinse in running tap water for 20 minutes. Dip in 91% alcohol. Transfer to 3% Hydrogen Peroxide and shake for 3 to 5 minutes for young explant material or 5 to 7 minutes for older explant material. Transfer to 250 ml of 10% bleach solution with one drop of baby shampoo as a surfactant. Shake for 5 to 10 minutes. Rinse in sterile water twice under your hood and transfer to your media.

Initiation

1 liter of distilled water
1/3 strength Murashige & Skoog (MS) Basal Salt Mixture
1 mg/ml of BAP (omit if using seeds)
1 ml of PPM
5 grams of Agar
30 grams of table sugar or sucrose
2-3 drops of food coloring for easy identification
pH adjusted to 5.6 - 5.8

Many plants will root when the BAP is exhausted so there may be no need to go to the multiplication or rooting stage. Simply divide and replate in new media or Harden off.

Multiplication

1 liter of distilled water
1/3 strength Murashige & Skoog (MS) Basal Salt Mixture
.5 mg/ml of Kinetin
1 ml of PPM
5 grams of Agar
30 grams of table sugar or sucrose
2-3 drops of food coloring for easy identification
pH adjusted to 5.6 - 5.8

Rooting

1 liter of distilled water
1/3 strength Murashige & Skoog (MS) Basal Salt Mixture
.1 mg/ml of IBA
1 ml of PPM
5 grams of Agar
30 grams of table sugar or sucrose
2-3 drops of food coloring for easy identification
pH adjusted to 5.6 - 5.8

Hardening

Divide rooted plantlets into individual plants or small groups. Using a 1:1 ratio of peat and coarse sand place plantlets in media using either plastic storage bins with a lid or nursery 1020 trays with cells and humidity dome. Gradually open lids to acclimate to room humidity.

Making Media

Media is the backbone of a plant tissue culture project. Some type of media is used in every stage of propagating plants. Media is used for initiation, multiplication, callus, and possibly even rooting. After a few batches, it will become second nature. Making batches of media will get much faster but in the beginning, seems like a daunting task.

Use a dedicated pot with a well-fitting lid to heat up media. When heating media make sure that the sucrose (table sugar) and the agar are heated properly. If the sucrose and the agar are not heated properly they will not mix evenly throughout the media properly and it will not be of suitable quality.

For ease of use, the standard of one liter of media is widely used. Scale this up or down depending on your needs. Get the protocol for the plant species that you're culturing handy. This will be your guide for making your media.

The first step is to get all of the components gathered and measured.

Measure out dry ingredients and place them into paper condiment cups. Measure out pre-made media like Murashige and Skoog for making one liter and set it aside. Measure out the amount of sugar needed and put it aside. Do the same with agar and keep it separate until it is heated. If protocol calls for any other dry ingredients measure them out on a scale and put them aside in paper condiment cups.

Pour about a half-liter of distilled water into a one liter graduated container as the first step. In a half-liter of distilled water put in the auxin or cytokinin using a pipette, per protocol requirements.

Add PPM (Plant Preservative Mixture) if using to prevent fungus or mold. Any other liquid ingredients can be added at this time as

Media supplies all the right components to influence your plants throughout the stages of their culture. Popular media inclused MS, agar, plant growth regulators, and sucrose. *Photo by Edward Johnson*

well. If using a stir plate start the container with a magnet stirrer and turn it on.

Using food coloring in media can help quickly and easily tell what media it is. Add one or two drops of food coloring to the media. Use the standard pack from the baking aisle at the grocery store. Designated colors for various media can help stop confusion about what the media is for. It doesn't matter what colors you use as long as you're consistent and remember what the color codes are. There are usually color recommendations on the food coloring pack. Make note of the number of drops and what colors to designate to a particular media.

Pick a color for the initiation stage, a color for multiplication, etc., and also make combinations of colors using those four basic colors. Separate colors for carnivorous plants and another for cryptocorynes, for example, may prove helpful.

Vary concentrations of the same color for initiation, multiplication, and callus. One drop, two drops, or three drops of color makes it easy to tell what it's for and what stage it's for quickly and easily.

Slowly add in the proper amount of powdered MS (Murashige and Skoog) or other medium being used. The protocol will tell how much to use. When a designation like 1/2 MS is not used full strength should be used. The weight for full strength is on the bottle and those measurements should be followed. Let it mix on the stir plate or stir manually with a spoon until dissolved.

Add in sugar or sucrose and stir slowly until all is dissolved into the media solution.

Do not add the agar at this time. Testing the pH of media with agar may create problems with the pH meter gumming up and making it hard to clean or possibly cause damage. Agar does not alter media very much in terms of pH. Add the agar last when the media is on the stove heated to boiling to ensure it gels properly.

Every single time the pH meter is used to test your media it must be calibrated. Every pH meter has its own procedure for checking and adjusting the meter properly. Most require turning on the meter, rinsing it in tap water, and putting it in either the high or low pH test liquid. Most often these are pH 4 and pH 7.

Suppose the pH meter starts with a pH 7 solution for calibrating. The pH meter is then put into the pH 7 liquid, as an example, and using the set screw to adjust the meter until it reads seven in the solution. Rinse in tap water and do the same with pH 4 testing liquid. Calibrating tests the meter to make sure the pH meter is accurate. It should be done each time a batch of media is made to ensure results are uniform and accurate.

Now that the pH meter is properly adjusted place it into the media. Be careful not to drop the pH meter too deeply into the liquid and ruin the meter. Let the meter sit for a few seconds and swirl around. Dip up-and-down gently to get a reading.

Aim for 5.8 for the pH for medium. Plants do best at this pH. Uptake of nutrients is best in this range of pH and it promotes optimum growth and uptake of nutrients. A few points off is not terrible. A reading of 5.4 to 6.0 is acceptable for the majority of plants needing 5.8 pH. Most plants will do fine with close readings. It is when the pH is 4.2 or 9.8 when there is a problem.

If the pH is too high or too low it can easily be adjusted. Vinegar and baking soda can be used to raise or lower pH. More often than not pH will be in the low 4 range. A small amount of baking soda can be used to bring the pH up to 5.6 to 5.8. It takes very little vinegar or baking soda in a liter of media to drastically change the pH.

The best method is to use a toothpick slightly moistened and dipped into baking soda. Next, dip the toothpick end into the media and continue to stir. Go slowly as it can take very little to make a big difference.

Rinse your pH meter in tap water and check your pH again. If it is still too low add more baking soda. If it is too high add vinegar using the same toothpick method. It is better to do too little at a time than have to go back and forth with vinegar and baking soda to get it right.

PH can greatly influence the growth of your plants. Most plants have an optimum range of pH that they will growth the most. Aim to stay within this pH range the best you can to promote the best growth and health. Photo by Edward Johnson

Once media pH is in the 5.6 to 5.8 range begin heating up the media on the stove or burner keeping the lid on to prevent evaporation. Medium heat is best.

Bring the covered media to a low boil. Ensure that all sucrose or sugar has been dissolved. Add in the agar a little at a time while stirring. If all the agar is added in at one time it will take quite a while to get dissolved and may get lumpy. Stir until it is dissolved evenly. Let the media boil for 30 seconds and turn off the heat.

Have your test tubes or jars nearby and ready to distribute your boiling hot media. Put about 1 inch of media into the bottom of each vessel. Pouring hot media takes caution not to get burned. A large plastic syringe will make it easy and make vessel volumes uniform. Large syringes can be found in the cooking section for injecting spices for turkeys or ordered online.

After media is added to each vessel it's time to put lids on. Make sure lids are threaded onto the jar properly. Once snug, back them off one-fourth of a turn. If tightened completely when they come out of the autoclave or pressure cooker they may be too tight to easily get off. They may also explode inside the autoclave or pressure cooker if they don't vent. They're now ready to be put into the autoclave or pressure cooker.

Explant Sterilization

Plant material to be initiated much be first sterilized. It must be done thoroughly but without killing the plant material. Any contaminates left on the explant will quickly result in fungus and mold in the prime environment of a jar of media.

To have the best success with a sterile explant start with the youngest cleanest material obtainable. The older the plant material is the more likely it is to be heavily contaminated. Fortunately, older and hardier plant material can usually handle harsher sterilization methods.

For some plants that are hard to get sterile it can be as simple as covering with a plastic bag and letting fresh new plant material grow. This is not always an option but this method can provide great results. Once enough new plant material has grown inside the protection of the clear plastic it can be used for explant material.

Some plant species have their particular protocol that works best for them. Many plants however will not have a protocol published in scientific papers. The vast majority of plants can be sterilized using the same protocol though. Some plants will just have to be experimented with before being successful.

Try, and try again. It may take one or two more times before getting a clean explant free of contaminates. It will have been worth the extra effort.

Start by getting explant material from the youngest and cleanest sources that are possible. It is best to cut a larger portion of the explant than is needed, as the plant will wick some of the alcohol and bleach into the cut ends. Later, remove the very ends that may have absorbed bleach or alcohol. This is a safety measure and may not always need to be done but is a simple insurance. If sterilants are wicked into the cutting they will turn to mush and die. A small amount of extra effort now will pay off later.

Using a plastic deli tub with a stainless steel tea strainer on top initial cleaning can be performed. The strainer must not let the plant material float up and out the top. Place the plant material in the deli tub and the stainless steel strainer on top of the tub. Place the deli tub under the kitchen sink and turn on the tap water.

Turn the water on just enough to keep the explant tumbling and swirling gently. Movement should not become so violent it damages the plant material. Many scientific papers say to leave your material tumbling in the tap water for 20 or 30 minutes. Success can be had with only five or six minutes if done thoroughly with lightly contaminated plants. Turn the water off when they are sufficiently cleaned.

Into the deli tub squirt one pump of anti-bacterial soap and let it sit for 15 minutes after gently agitating. After rinsing again in tap water remove the strainer and pour some of the water off so the tub isn't filled.

Still in the tap water take the new explant into the lab area next to your clean hood. With a pair of tweezers or forceps remove the explant and dip it into rubbing alcohol for about 30 seconds.

The preferred method is a small glass jar with a tight fitting lid. Put the explant into the alcohol jar half filled with alcohol and shake it gently. A 100 ml jar or a small baby food jar will work fine. Make sure the lid is secure and does not leak. Use caution not to get alcohol or other liquid into eyes, skin, or on other surfaces.

Alcohol is a harsh sterilant for many plants so avoid killing the plant by leaving it in too long. Take out the explant and rinse in clean tapwater.

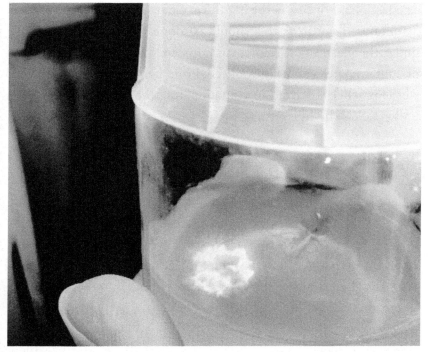

Improperly sterilized plant material will begin to grow mold or fungus. It is best to start with multiple explants to best increase your odds of getting a clean culture for initiation.

Next, a 3% solution of hydrogen peroxide is used to further clean the explant. Soak the explant in the hydrogen peroxide for 3 to 5 minutes. For larger pieces it can soak for 8 or 9 minutes. Use a small jar half filled with hydrogen peroxide and shake the explant continuously. Setting a timer is a good way to ensure of sterilization times.

Using a 10% solution of bleach put about 200 ml into another glass jar and place the explant inside. Baby shampoo is added to the solution as a surfactant. Use four or five drops in the 200 ml of bleach solution. The jar is capped and then shaken for about five or six minutes. Large explants or particularly dirty explants can be shaken for 8 to 10 minutes.

The last phase of this is rinsing the explants in sterile water for 3 to 5 minutes. Two times this should be done. Do this last sterilizing under the clean hood using sterile forceps and a sterile clean hood or contaminates will be introduced. From here on explants will need sterile practices to avoid re-contaminating the explant and working under a clean hood is a must.

To sterilize the hood use a spray bottle with a 10% bleach solution. Put on latex or nitrile gloves. Using the finest sprayer mist possible moisten the inside of the hood with a fine even layer of bleach solution. It does not need to be soaking wet or dripping.

Everything that goes into or under the clean hood must be sprayed with bleach or otherwise sterilized before going into the clean hood. There are no exceptions..

Spray each gloved hand gently but thoroughly to sterilize them. Rub gloved hands together to make sure every bit of surface is covered. Hold the forceps and scalpel under the hood and spray them with the bleach solution. Place them on a small plate that has been sprayed with bleach solution inside the hood or store them in a jar of 10% bleach solution.

Carefully, holding the explant in the hood which is still in its container of 10% bleach solution spray the outside of the explant jar. Once moistened with bleach solution set it inside the bleach moistened hood. Spray two jars of sterile water completely as well as the jar or jars of initiation media you will be putting the new explants into. Every single item that goes into the hood must be sterilized.

Use a face mask at the hood because it keeps exhalation from entering inside of the hood, especially not using a laminar flow-through hood. Breathing into the clean hood carries outside air currents into your workspace which is something you want to avoid. Always open jars away from the front of the clean hood. Do not open sterile jars outside the clean hood.

If hands begin to dry out from bleach solution gently spray them again. It is nearly as successful to keep the bleach sprayer right next to the hood as it is to keep it inside of the hood. Spray gloved hands every time they are removed from the clean hood and rub them togeher while still wet with bleach spray before putting them back under the hood.

The only thing that can or should be touched outside of the hood while plating up is the bottle of bleach. Do so very carefully. If hands are constantly moist with bleach solution there should be little to worry about. Unless plating a lot at one time there should only be a need to spray your hands one time though.

If for any reason hands are taken out out of the hood they must be sprayed with bleach solution before putting them back into the hood.

There are no exceptions to this practice. It is important to maintain clean hands. This has been repeated because it is key to success when curbing contamination in vessels and explants.

Carefully, still with bleach moistened gloved hands, get the forceps and rinse them in sterile water. Pull out the explant and place it into a jar of sterile water to rinse for 3 to 5 minutes. Agitate it gently like all the other previous steps.

When done, carefully rinse the scalpel in sterile water and remove the explant from its first jar of sterile water. Trim the end or ends of the explant to remove any tissue that may have soaked up bleach or alcohol solution. Do this carefully and place the explant into the sec-

Old or heavily contaminated plants can be grown inside individual containers or in plastic storage bins to obtain cleaner growth. Once new growth occurs take this new less infested material to use for getting clean explants. Photo by Edward Johnson

ond jar of sterile water. Close the jar and agitate it for 3 to 5 minutes. It is now ready to be put into your initiation jar of media.

Ideally, place one single explant into its initiation vessel. This is the highest stage of contamination and reducing the number of explants in each vessel with increase the chances of getting a clean and viable initiation culture. Test tubes and smaller vessels are best suited for this purpose.

Once done placing explant material into initiation media remove the newly plated initiation jars and label clearly and fully. Rinse all tools in clean tapwater and dry them. Wipe down the inside of the clean hood with a paper towel and cover it or turn it facing down to dry.

There are of course other protocols that can be used to sterilize explant material. Constantly look for new ways that take less time and effort.

Consider using a magnetic stir plate to save time shaking jars. The spinning magnet underneath makes the magnetic stir bar in the jar of sterilant spin and creates a vortex which cleans the explant. NaDCC and other gentle sterilants can be used for long periods to gently sterilize delicate plants.

This is a very efficient method of sterilizing explant material. Longer periods of gentle agitation in a lower concentration of bleach can be very effective for hard to sterilize plants. Major benefits can be seen with aquatic plants and plants that have been collected from outside.

There are many ways to go about sterilizing explant materials. Alcohol, bleach, NaDCC, hydrogen peroxide, or other sterilants may be used. What matters is a sterile and healthy explant. Combinations of sterilants and various time schedules are key to finding clean explants. Repeatedly contaminated explants or explants that did not survive initiation should be tried again with another protocol or sterilant.

With explant initiations that repeatedly grow contamination try again with longer soaking times. Consider a lower concentration of sterilant and longer soak times. Try longer pre-rinse times. Also look for cleaner explant material or wait until new growth has produced enough clean material for another tray with the explant.

If explants rapidly turn black or deteriorate quickly try a more mild protocol for sterilizing. Many plants cannot survive long alcohol or bleach dips. Try physically longer or larger explant material and trim

Explants are taken from plants and trimmed into manageable sizes. Initial cleanings can be done with larger portions of the explant remaining intact. Cutting stems before soaking in alcohol and bleach solutions can damage plants through capillary action. Photo by Edward Johnson

away more before the final rinse and plating. Try trimming more of the excess after the final rinse.

Don't give up when failure comes. Try different methods if there is no published protocol. Look for similar plants that do have protocols published and try to adapt them to fit the explant. If it is difficult, likely, the plant isn't being offered for sale from tissue culture by others. Eventually sucess will come with this stage.

There are other simple tricks but many are not as successful. Supersonic jewelry cleaners work well to blast off contamiation with subsonic blasts. Cinnamon and turmeric added to soaking water will also help clean explants of contaminates and is worth exploring.

Always be on the lookout for new ideas for sterilization. Try different protocols, sterilants, soaking times, and eventually success will be found.

Sterilizing Seeds

Seeds are a great way to get new plants into tissue culture. Seeds offer genetic diversity so they should be used for species plants, not cultivars or sports. Cultivars and sports that produce seed will not usually produce the same results as the parent plant which produced the seed.

Seeds are often easily available through mail order and are easier to store than cuttings. Collecting seeds is an easy method to obtain new species and to find new cultivars. Trading is also a popular way to grow your plant species collection.

Sterilizing seed isn't difficult with a few tricks. Larger seeds are relatively easy and straight forward. Tiny seeds are hard to work with and some seeds, like nepenthes, can be tricky.

Small seeds can be placed in empty teabags available at most grocery stores adding a staple on the top after folding. This secures them safely for the washing process. Run tap water over them for 10 minutes as a prewash just like any other explant cleansing method. Use caution not to break open the teabag.

Hardy seeds can be washed for as long as 20 minutes in a 10 percent bleach solution. Drop the teabag with seeds into a container and soak. Shake vigorously periodically. Not all seed needs to be rinsed in sterile water. Remove the seeds carefully from the teabag and plate them into initiation media vessels under the clean hood.

For non-hardy species try a clean hood rinse in sterile water for 3 minutes at least one time before plating into initiation vessels. Some hardy seeds can endure the extra sterilant but many cannot. Leaving sterilant on nonhardy species will kill them.

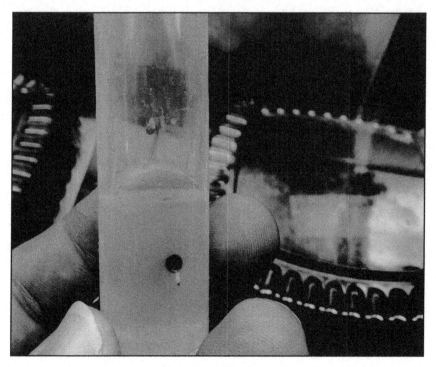

Seeds are often durable and can withstand heavy cleaning in bleach resulting in clean explant material. Seed, however, is not always genetically stable and you may or may not get the plant you wanted especially with cultivars. Photo by Edward Johnson

Large seeds can be washed without having to secure them in a tea-bag. Metal tea balls that split in half can come in handy for cleaning larger seeds. Run them under tap water for 10 to 20 minutes as a pre-clean. Follow up with a rinse in bleach or other disinfectants. If the seed needs to be rinsed in sterile water do so before plating.

Using either 10 percent bleach or 3 percent hydrogen peroxide for delicate seeds soak them for 3 to 10 minutes. Rinse in sterile water under the hood. Delicate seeds should be rinsed as many as 3 times in sterile water.

Some seeds that are heavily contaminated can be sterilized using an overnight sugar water soak. The sugar water encourages fungus and bacteria to grow making it more susceptible to hydrogen peroxide or bleach soaking the following day. Drain off the sugar water and soak in 10 percent bleach or 3 percent hydrogen peroxide (or other sterilants) for 10 minutes. Some hardy seeds do not need to be rinsed in sterile water and can be placed in initiation media with just a hydrogen peroxide or light bleach solution rinse.

Many published protocols will have the process used to get seeds sterile for initiation. Sometimes more steps are needed and it is necessary to become creative. Using the teabag method with various soaks, the sugar water soak, and other methods will test your patience but results are usually only a step away from the last failed attempt.

Use these tips and processes interchangeably when failures occur. Increase or decrease soak times and change the sterilant used. Instead of bleach try hydrogen peroxide or brief 91 percent alcohol dips.

Some seeds need special circumstances to germinate and begin to grow. Some plants require stratification from cold, fire, or damage to the seed shell in the form of scarification.

Most of these requirements can be artificially manipulated with plant growth regulators. Cold stratifying seeds can often simply be placed in the freezer for a couple of months. Many will germinate after being soaked in a GA3 plant growth regulator solution.

Hard seeds that need scarifying can be sanded with a nail file to encourage germination. Some seeds can be cracked and opened to encourage germination after sterilization or before being sterilized. It is normally better to open seeds and sterilize them without the hull or husk.

Research each species before attempting to initiate into a culture to

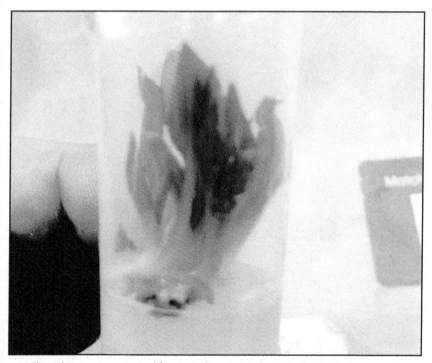

These hosta were started from seed contained within this initiation vessel. While seed don't always produce the same offspring as the motherplant they can be a great way to grow species or variations. Photo by Edward Johnson

make sure there are no special requirements for that species of plant. If it never germinates because it wasn't properly stratified it doesn't matter if it is sterilized.

Seeds such as those from open-pollinated hostas can be interesting to tissue culture from the sheer variety of plant variations from one seed pod to the next. Even seeds from the same pod can produce a variety of leaf shapes and colors.

Seeds are generally not difficult to sterilize and can provide an excellent source for new plant species to begin a new culture. Don't overlook seeds as a source for initiation and don't get discouraged if you fail at first.

Sterilizing Vessels

Sterilizing tissue culture tools and vessels of media is a very important procedure. Conditions in each jar of media are optimal for mold and fungus growing so they must be sterilized to avoid them growing in your jars.

Sterilizing vessels involves placing them into an autoclave or pressure cooker at a high enough temperature for some time. As an alternative, a microwave can also be used for smaller batches.

Water boils at 212° F at atmospheric pressure. This is not hot enough to kill most contaminants. However, when the autoclave or pressure cooker increases the internal pressure water will boil at a much higher temperature.

With a pressure cooker, 230° F can easily be reached, which is hot enough to kill contaminants in the media for our use and purpose.

Autoclaves meant for medical and lab use are quite expensive. Even a small autoclave meant only for hand tools can cost more than $1000. Luckily, kitchen style pressure cookers meant for home canning can be used with satisfactory results.

Today's pressure cooker has several safety features that make them quite safe to use. Most pressure cookers operate with the same basic function but you need to make sure you have read and understood the instructions for your particular pressure cooker.

Several readily available models are available in 23-quart size. 23 quarts is a good size for a batch of tissue culture vessels for home tissue culture use.

Around 20 to 25 baby food jars will fit into a 23-quart pressure cooker. Always make sure your pressure cooker is clean inside and out. Look for any dents. Inspect the lids' seal to make sure it is free of damage. There is a stem where the weight sits on, hold the lid up to the light, and look through to make sure the hole is clear and not obstructed. Check any rubber fittings or safety features to be sure they're seated properly. Follow the manufacturers' instructions for use and safety.

Once you are satisfied everything on your pressure cooker is in good working order you will need to place the rack in the bottom of the pressure cooker. Do not place glass jars directly on the bottom of the pressure cooker. With the bottom rack in place pour just enough water to come up to the underside of the rack. Do not overfill so that water can touch the bottom of the jars.

Carefully place jars evenly spaced around the bottom of the pressure cooker. Leave space between each jar to encourage even temperatures inside. Stacking multiple layers is perfectly fine. When stacking jars or vessels make sure they are secure and not prone to falling over.

Pressure cookers can be used instead of autoclaves to sterilize vessels. Autoclaves are often cost prohibitive to use, especially in the beginning before any returns start coming in from plants produced. Photo by Edward Johnson

With the pressure cooker loaded with vessels, place the lid on. Do not put the pressure weight on the lid yet. Place the pressure cooker on the stove and set the burner to medium heat. Leave the weighted cap off the pressure cooker until everything is heated up thoroughly. Wait until a steady stream of steam is coming out of the weight stem for several minutes.

Once the pressure cooker has begun making a steady stream of steam you can now put the weight on the stem. It should take several minutes before the weight will start rocking back and forth letting steam escape. The weight controls the pressure inside of the pressure cooker. When too much pressure builds up inside the cooker the weight allows it to be released safely. You should get a pretty even tempo of the weight releasing steam making it rock back and forth.

Once the weight begins rocking back and forth and releasing steam at an even pace you can begin the timer for 23 minutes (if using baby food jars with about 25 mL of media).

Sterilization time varies on each quantity of media in each vessel. 100 ml of media is not going to reach the same temperature as 25 mL of media in the same amount of time. Adjust times for larger quantities of media. Larger volumes may need several extra minutes to achieve sterilization.

Once the timer goes off simply turn the burner on the stove off. Do not open the pressure cooker at this time. Do not remove the

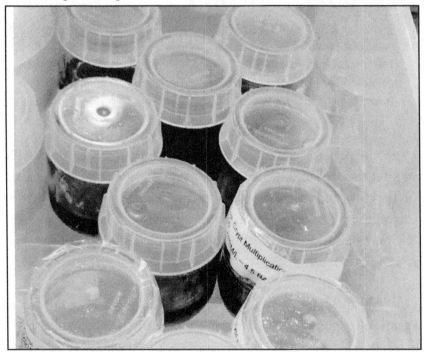

Vessels must be sterilized after it has been filled. Once sterilized care must be taken to only open under the safety of the hood. Sterility must be maintained throughout the entire process for success. Photo by Edward Johnson

weight. Allow the pressure cooker to come back to room temperature at its own pace. This can take an hour or more but do not aid in the cooling process. Wait until it is cool to the touch before opening the pressure cooker. Do so carefully and only near your clean box or plastic storage bins.

Protect newly sterilized vessels from contamination. Placing them in an area where there is a large temperature difference can cause contamination because the vessel's air inside of the jar cools and draws in outside air. The best place is a constant steady temperature out of direct sunlight or drafts.

Using plastic storage bins to keep sterilized vessels can help prevent contamination. A lid on the bins keeps dust and other contamination from falling on the vessel's lid and possibly being drawn in through temperature differences. Spray in a fine mist of 10% bleach before putting your vessels in if contamination problems occur from environmental contaminants.

Place the newly sterilized jars in immediately upon opening the pressure cooker lid. Take the storage bins where they are stored or used. Even though you have been very careful you must still spray them with a bleach solution or alcohol before putting them into your clean hood to plate up new plant material. Air has many contaminants floating around.

Microwaving medium is another option for sterilizing. Small batches of media in the microwave may be more convenient. Microwaving more than two or three vessels at a time can become tedious, however. It isn't suggested to use the microwave for more than 2 or 3 vessels at a time as it is a tedious process.

Arrange vessels evenly on a plate and place them into the microwave. Each microwave is different and power settings are different from model to model. Boil the media for three minutes. Turn the microwave on and when it starts to boil up toward the top turn it off. Then turn it back on. Then turn it back off. Sitting in front of the microwave pushing the On/Off button is the best way to regulate the boiling so that it does not boil over or remain too cool.

Microwaving is tedious and doesn't always work. For this reason, it isn't recommended for beginners. After some experience with microwaving it can be suitable to sterilize two or three jars for a particular reason.

Microwaving can save time but it isn't efficient for a lot of vessels. Pressure cooker or autoclave is more thorough and you will by default have vessels that are still contaminated and will grow fungus and mold. Starting, this can prove discouraging. If a pressure cooker or autoclave isn't available a microwave can provide sterilization but it is not an ideal method.

Plating and Replating Cultures

Plating and replating cultures are much the same as when creating initiation cultures. Everything must be sterile. Replating is simply taking one mature or ready culture and dividing it into multiple new vessels. These can later be grown out or replated for even more cultures.

It is very important not to contaminate vessels when putting plant material into sterile jars. Always wear gloves and always use proper techniques to avoid contaminating plantlets or explants. As in almost all other steps of tissue culture keep everything sterile and work carefully.

Keep tools and vessels under the clean hood at all times. When removing tools or hands from under the clean box make sure to resterilize them. Avoid breathing into the clean box by wearing a facemask to prevent airflow from pushing air into your sterile workplace.

Sterilize your box properly beforehand and get all your needed tools and vessels handy. Sterilize your hands and any jars or tools going into the hood. Make sure you have all you need in the clean box before sitting down to replate.

Use a spray bottle with 10% bleach solution to wet the inside of the clean hood thoroughly. A fine mist should cover all inside surfaces of the clean hood. Spray your gloved hands to wet them thoroughly and wipe your hands together to ensure coverage. Spray each item lightly but wet the entire surface before placing jars, tools, and other equipment into the clean hood.

Place your new jars on one rear side under your clean hood, and your jars to be replated on the other. Keep things neat and tidy without

These deli tubs are ready to go onto the growing rack. Old multiplication vessels have been split up and some plantlets have been held back for new multiplication vessels. The others have gone to grow out. Photo by Edward Johnson

clutter. Work quickly, but methodically. You will learn to open and close the lids with one hand while keeping the forceps from touching anything else.

When opening jars to remove plantlets or explants keep them at a slight angle toward you. Use this same method for new vessels when transferring plant material. Avoid touching the sides of the jars or vessels, the clean box, or any other surface. If you feel like you have compromised your tools resterilize them under the box in a container of bleach or other similar sterilants. Keep working under the box until you are finished.

Work with one jar at a time. Do not open multiple new jars at once to save time. This is a means to introduce contaminants into your

Culture of aquarium dwarf hairgrass ready to be replated. This one jar of Eleocharis parvula will create about two dozen new culture jars which will each grow into what you see here. Photo by Edward Johnson

new jars. It is common to remove plantlets from multiplication, or callus, and cut them up into small pieces on a plate but do not open more than one new jar at a time. Avoid working directly over a mass of plantlets if you avoid it. Place your multiplication mass of plants further to the rear of the clean hood to reduce the chance of contaminants falling into the plantlets.

Carefully place your plant material into your new vessel, whether it be multiplication media, callus media, or rooting media. Put the lid on and screw it down and move on to the next vessel until you are finished. Keep your groups of media together and orderly to avoid confusion and contamination.

Bleach your tools inside the clean hood between vessels by using two jars of bleach in 10% and 1% concentrations. Quickly dip your tool into the 10% bleach solution and twirl gently and rinse in the 1% solution before moving to the next vessel. Some delicate species you may need to rinse in sterile water after the bleach dip. 250 ppm Na-DCC solution is good to use for sterilizing as it is more gentle than bleach. If you have to get up and walk away from the clean hood workspace place your tools in the bleach until you return. Thoroughly clean your hands again before resuming work.

When you are finished carefully check the lids to make sure they are snug but not overly tight while still under the clean box. Use plastic kitchen cling wrap around the lids to help seal out contaminants as they are removed from the clean hood. Place them into plastic totes with lids that have been lightly sprayed with either alcohol, a bleach solution, or some similar sterilant. Stack your boxes on your lighted racks and clean your box and other tools. Rinse all tools and vessels with tapster and allow to air dry. Dispose of old media properly.

Initiation Stage

Initiation is the first stage in plant tissue culture. This stage will take necessary plant material from a donor plant, called an explant, and place them in appropriate media. Chemicals and substances in the media encourage this plant material to survive and begin to grow.

Typically, the initiation phase uses very little plant growth regulators. Make sure that the explant is sterile and becomes accustomed to its new environment. The initiation stage is meant to get the explant comfortable and as stress-free as possible in its new conditions. Some plants will successfully initiate and multiply with only this media. Too many plant growth regulators can slow growth or even kill the explant.

Success with initiation requires patience and dedication. It is, perhaps, the hardest stage of plant tissue culture. Most likely contaminated vessels and fungus or mold issues will plague cultures, to begin with. Don't be discouraged and quit. Once past any initial setbacks, progress will quickly be achieved.

Shoots are cut and sterilized as explants before being put into the initiation phase. These shoots are growing nicely in their new home. Soon they will begin to proliferate and help make hundreds or thousands of new plantlets. Photo by Edward Johnson

Initiation media should be spread out over more and smaller vessels than the other stages. Since initiation typically doesn't stay in for months at a time smaller media volume is possible.

Having more and smaller vessels allows you to more freely try to get more clean cultures started. It is not uncommon to try several times to get a clean uncontaminated culture from initiation.

Many first attempts will result in fuzzy mold or fungus and have to be disposed of. Occasionally, contaminated cultures can be saved but it is not the norm.

Different sterilizing protocols should be tried until one is found that works. Notes should be taken to keep track of success in the event cultures down the line become contaminated or otherwise die. Mishaps can occur and cultures can be lost.

More initiation vessels will be used than one may think. It makes sense to try to sterilize several pieces of plant material at once because many things can lead to failures. When tissue culturing a plant it is better to try three or five pieces than only one. Ideally, more than one explant of the same plant will be sterilized and put into its sterilization vessel. It will save time in the long run and lead to more multiplication vessels to work with.

Using test tube type containers uses far less media than baby food jars or other larger vessels. This means more containers, more initiated cultures, and more explants using less media.

This is the stage that most find most difficult. Many contaminated explants and mold growing jars will be encountered and there will be setbacks. Keep trying! Pay attention to processes and learn the best way to initiate certain plants using particular methods that coax them into a culture.

Do not let setbacks from contamination slow down your enthusiasm. This is perhaps the most difficult stage to pass, especially when first learning. It may not be your fault as some plants have contaminants inside their structure. Keep trying until a clean explant is created.

Once the explant material is showing signs of growth it can be replated into multiplication media. Commonly, new growth can be seen inside the vessel. New growth shows that the plant has acclimated well and it is ready to move along to the next stage. Some plants take days, some weeks, and some even longer. If one doesn't start growing place it on the grow-out rack and wait. If it doesn't die and isn't contaminated try to plate it into multiplication.

Multiplication Stage

Explants that are doing well in initiation media can be replated into multiplication vessels. Initiation should take two or three weeks to make sure it is not contaminated. Once established initiation cultures grow without contamination it can go into the multiplication stage.

Multiplication is one of the most exciting parts of plant tissue culture. Lots of new little plantlets are coming up and splitting off. Masses of plantlets begin to grow and fill the jars. This is the stage where exponential growth happens. Single little explants now become three, five, or even more new plants. Once strong multiplication appears in jars you know you're almost there.

Some plants will multiply on their own simply in initiation media. These plants are far and few between generally though (many carnivorous plants are good candidates for this). Cytokinins in media are largely responsible for our new burst of growth. Cytokinins help create new growth in the form of shoots for clumps of new plantlets.

The most amazing thing about this stage is when the new clump of plants is ready to be divided and replated. A clump of 10 new plantlets can easily be found, often more. Now use these plants to create new vessels which will make more new plantlets each. Continue growing, dividing, and multiplying these plants, potentially limitless. One plant can turn into ten, then one hundred, and on to thousands.

The best plan is to multiply plantlets until a goal of production is met. Choose a realistic number to keep in multiplication production. Perhaps create one thousand plants a month to run the multiplication stage. Once you have your one hundred jars with explants which will be producing one thousand plants, all extra will be either put into rooting or grown out and potted up for sale or trade. Simply adjust the number of vessels by how many plantlets come from each vessel. Simple math.

To increase or decrease production, easily do so by how many vessels are running in the cycle. If more plants are needed then create more multiplication jars. If fewer plants are desired take more plants out of multiplication. It's simple and easy.

Many plants will multiply and begin to grow roots as the cytokinins are used up in the jars of multiplication media. With attention to this, adjusting cytokinin levels in media can help this along. High levels of cytokinin may create a huge mass of new plantlets but it can inhibit root growth. This may not even be a problem as many plants can be rooted easily in nursery trays or plastic bins.

To encourage root growth in the multiplication stage, try lowering the amount of multiplication slightly with your cytokinins. This may take a little experimentation by lowering increments of cytokines. Use one milligram per liter less or half a milligram per liter less of cytokinin in your media. Take notes on plants and media concerning

Multiplication is the most exciting stage in plant tissue culture. Massive amounts of plantlets in each vessel will exponentially lead to more. Real progress can be made once this stage is attained. Photo by Edward Johnson

plantlet creation and rooting progress. Note the number of plantlets produced and how many days it takes until rooting until you reach a happy zone. Alternatively, multiplication vessels can be left in a culture much longer than necessary until plantlets begin to fill the gelled media with rootlets. Too much time in the media though and plantlets will deteriorate and die rapidly.

It may not always be possible to time plantlet growth with a vessel running out of cytokinin to creating roots. When it does though it will omit a step and save time and effort. It may seem like a lot of effort, in the beginning, to keep notes on plantlet creation and rooting but when an entire stage is skipped it saves a lot of time. Adjust amounts of plants produced by adding more or fewer jars to meet the production goals set earlier.

Some plants seem to exhaust themselves in multiplication when re-plated numerous times. When and if the production of new plantlets slows down to unacceptable levels they may need to be reinitiated with new explants. Some species of plants can be replated into initiation media and left to grow more slowly. This can coax more out of the current batch of explants and extend their cultured usefulness. Not all plants do this, however, and it is not all that common for it to happen.

Producing vessels with acceptable multiplication can be assuring that the path to success is ahead. Even when success is clear pay attention to protocols and a sterile environment. Success is hinged on the ability to pay attention to detail, repeat outcomes repeatedly, and stick with practices that create clean vessels without contamination. Continue to quickly remove any contaminated vessels from the growing area to prevent further vessel contamination. Keep multiplication vessels covered from dust and excessive temperature swings and keep moving forward with production.

Callus Stage

Callus is undifferentiated cells forming into a mass of cells. It often looks like tiny hair-like leaves, small plantlets, or just some green disfigured mass. It is the strangest stage of tissue culture. It is similar to the multiplication stage in that it is used to grow a lot of plant material.

Callus is a growth of cells that don't have any particular purpose yet. This mass of cells is undifferentiated and is not growing roots or shoots. Callus can be grown with little or no light because it does not photosynthesize. It can be manipulated with plant growth regulators to make shoots and or roots. This is why it is valuable in plant tissue culture.

Like the multiplication stage where a bundle of plantlets can be divided callus can also be divided. There are no plantlets but the mass can be taken out of callus stage and divided just like with multiplication.

Jars of callus can be used to make even more jars of callus. They also can be replated into new media to make them grow roots and shoots.

To turn one vessel of callus into 5 or 10 new vessels of callus to increase production simply replate them into new jars of callus media. In some ways, it is easier to divide up callus than it is to divide up a clump of very small plantlets. Simply repeat this process until you have enough jars to meet your production demands.

Using the proper plant growth regulators, callus can be made to grow shoots and or roots. Some callus stage cultures can be grown into plants without any plant growth regulators by letting the mass exhaust callus causing plant growth regulators. The vast majority of plants will need help with the proper plant growth regulators.

Callus is an odd stage as it forms a lump of undifferentiated plant material. From here it can be split up and made to shoot or further multiply. Photo by Edward Johnson

Try to avoid callus because it takes extra steps and some of the chemicals used to induce callus can also be more dangerous. Try to streamline plant tissue culture from start to finish.

If callus isn't productive for a particular species skip this stage. Re-plating extra stages of growth is not generally a timesaver. Some plants however will benefit and grow better when using a callus stage. Gains lost by not using the callus stage may be made up for by skipping the extra labor of this stage.

Most published protocols will have callus stage information for media and other details. It has its uses. Generally, this practice is just another step unless it proves productive results over a simple multiplication stage. To save time and resources go from initiation to multiplication and skip the callus stage if possible.

Grow Out Stage

Growing out plants propagated with tissue culture is similar to hardening off plants started from seed indoors using humidity domes. Plants that have been in an environment with excellent growing conditions need time to adjust to their new conditions. Cultured plants are delicate from having been grown in optimum conditions with very little stress.

One of the more delicate conditions to deal with when growing out plants is humidity. There is no need for a high-tech greenhouse with a misting system though. Use commonly available size 1020 plastic nursery trays with humidity domes or plastic shoe storage bins to harden off plants for potting up. Nursery trays with humidity domes or plastic storage bins can produce thousands of plants each month easily.

Nursery trays are very handy to use, especially with multi-celled tray inserts. There are many sizes available and prove to also be very neat and orderly. Humidity domes fit perfectly on them and some come with an adjustable vent to control humidity when hardening off new plantlets. The downfall is that the thin production 1020 trays are flimsy without a frame. 1020 nursery flats are also available in much heavier duty plastic but are also much more expensive.

Use the same style racks and lights that are used for tissue culture lighting racks. Standard nursery trays have several cell size options from large 15 count to small 98 cell count. Nursery trays aren't necessary and it is possible to use plastic storage totes with potting mix in the bottom.

Whether using nursery trays or a plastic storage bin it is important to use the right substrate. Some plants do better in species-specific substrates. Also, take into consideration that some plants will grow faster than others. Certain plants also will be better suited sold and shipped bare-rooted, without soil in the roots. Take these differences into consideration when choosing a substrate and method to grow out.

Rockwool is an excellent option for some aquatic plants like cryptocoryne and echinodorus which will grow an extensive root system relatively easily. Plants with strong root systems make healthy plants. Healthy plants are easy to sell and ship as well.

Stem plants do well with perlite and water as they are normally fast rooters and growers, but are sold bare-rooted and by the stem. It makes it easy to collect stems and bundle them for sale or transplant. Coarse sand and fine gravel or hydroton clay balls as a substrate for larger plants are also economical and effective.

After deflasking plants from the vessels of multiplication media use a scalpel or razor if needed and separate the plants into individual plantlets or small groups of plants. Rinse the agar off the plantlets gently. Place them into a small bin filled with tap water as you separate them to clean the roots. Once you have all your plants cut, cleaned, and divided they are ready to be planted out.

Perlite can be used to root many tissue cultured plantlets. A layer of perlite in a shoe bin or plastic tub with two inches of water can be very easy and effective. Perlite gives the plants support while allowing them to be in contact with water, but not submerged. This encourages root growth.

Some plants will not root well in perlite. Rooting hormones such as commercially available products can boost rooting significantly. Follow the product instructions like you would for any other cuttings. Using powdered plant growth regulators is also an option as they are already on hand for making media. Once they are rooted remove

Tissue cultured plants can either be sold off as liners to nurseries or grown out yourself. There are many methods to grow plants out for sale. Plants can be grown on racks or outside. Photo by Edward Johnson

Growing out plants can be a rewarding part of plant tissue culture. Plants that once took a great deal of time to propagate can now be done in quantity. Growers can quickly multiply their plant production exponentially. Photo by Edward Johnson

them and pot them up or sell them as rooted starts.

Forceps or tweezers work well for placing small plantlets into the substrate uniformly. The most economical and common method is a plastic storage bin with 2 inches of potting soil in the bottom. Place plantlets evenly spaced in a grid fashion for quick and easy work.

Wet the potting soil before planting the new plantlets. Dry potting soil can float up and make a mess of newly placed plantlets when watered. When this happens there will be an unmanageable mess. For aquatic plants, a thin layer of water covering the substrate can be tolerated and even encourage higher humidity for acclimating.

After planting, place the clear storage bin lid on and set it on the lighting rack for as long as a couple of weeks. Crack open the lid more and more after the first week to get the plantlets used to lower humidity. Keep an eye on them in case they dry out too quickly. If they dry out too much use a fine atomizer to mist them with water. Spritzing with a fine mist may be necessary more than once a day. Slow down spritzing as they acclimate and look like they are no longer suffering from being too dry.

Using this method of growing out and hardening off tissue cultured plants is easy and it works well. Don't worry if there's not an outdoor greenhouse. Growing plants out inside is an effective method to produce lots of healthy plants.

Some plants, like these cryptocorynes, need to be acclimated to room or greenhouse conditions slowly. Potting up clumps of plantlets taken from tissue culture and growing them out in plastic storage totes can be easy. This can be done inside and in the greenhouse. Photo by Edward Johnson

Plants that come from tissue culture need not worry about pests and snails. Growing plants out creates larger plants that are hardy to handle and ship. Grown out, there is no difference from plants available from any other source. Rooted and growing, any plant growth regulators have been metabolized by the plant.

Phenolic Exudates

Explants when initiated or when being multiplied, on occasion, can turn brown and become mushy. Phenolic exudant as it is known happens when the plant cells are exposed to an oxidant. Cutting the explant material exposes cells which in turn triggers an injury response. Brown mush isn't very appetizing to insects and other predators and this is what the plant is hoping for.

Some species and some certain explant material are more prone to phenolic exudates than others. Most plants introduced into plant tissue culture will do fine and can be cultured without problems. Others we must take extra steps in preparing the explant to get viable useable material and avoid them turning to mush.

Use actively growing shoot tips to ensure they are not dormant. Actively growing shoot tips are less likely to turn into mush than older established material might. New growth that is actively growing is also cleaner than older harder material which will require longer sterilization times that can affect explant health. Longer soaking times allow more time for sterilants like chlorine and alcohol to wick into the explant through the same capillary action that allows water to reach the plant's cells.

Transferring initiated explants often can beat the exudate cycle. Fungus and other contaminants most often show up within 5 to 7 days after initiation. Transfer the 'clean' and healthy explants to new media every 5 to 7 days until the browning stops.

Sensitive explants should not be cut into too small sections. If prone to brown and turn into mush cut your explants into larger pieces. Since the pieces of explant are larger this will allow trimming the cut ends shorter before plating. This removes plant cells that may have wicked in sterilants. Try sterilizing explant with NaDCC or vinegar/peroxide instead of bleach as it is more gentle on the plant material.

Reducing lighting periods can also help slow the browning of explants. When using BAP in media stay within 2mg/L to 5 mg/L if problems occur with exudate.

Charcoal put into media in the range of 0.5 to 2.0 grams per liter can help reduce browning and phenolic exudates. Charcoal darkens the media and supports root growth which can inhibit some types of growth when used with some plant growth regulators. It is best to get troublesome explants going without charcoal but if it isn't possible try charcoal in the range listed. Check pH levels before adding charcoal to make sure pH is in the 5.8 range. Check the pH again after adding the charcoal to ensure proper pH (but before adding agar).

Some plants have bacteria growing inside their tissue and this can create conditions for rapid browning. Shoot tips that grow fungus or mold at the cut section and turn brown may suffer from this. When this happens replate onto new media after trimming off browning areas (it may not be necessary to resterilize that particular explant). Larger than needed explant material can help with this as it allows trimming off browned areas and leaves enough explant material to continue growing.

Vitamin C can be added to the media to help combat the browning process. Vitamin C has been shown to deteriorate when autoclaved but tissue culture media that has Vitamin C added before autoclaving still has beneficial antioxidant properties. Adding from 20-50 mg/l of Vitamin C (ascorbic acid) before autoclaving can make it possible to get past the initiation stage. The media itself helps prevent browning but the explant must be pushed under the surface of the media to contact the Vitamin C. Adding Vitamin C can affect your gelling agent and you may need to adjust your media by adding

This culture media was beginning to turn brown. Once phenolic exudant starts it is best to approach the problem sooner than later. Replate or take other steps to protect the cultures. Photo by Edward Johnson

slightly more gelling agent usually by about 10 percent more.

Tablets or other forms of Vitamin C from pharmacy sources are readily available. Weigh the tablet or powder and subtract the amount of ascorbic acid in the tablet from the total weight (this can be found on the box label). A common Vitamin C tablet weighs 690 mg and contains 500 mg of Vitamin C. This shows there is 190 mg of additional ingredients in the tablet to be adjusted for.

The math: 500 (mg) divided by 690 (total weight) gives us .72463768 percent Vitamin C or about 72 percent. For 100 mg we would divide 100 by .72 and we would need to measure out 138.8 mg to get 100 mg of total Vitamin C.

Finally, as a last resort, cut explants while submerged in a solution of potassium citrate ($K_3C_6H_5O_7$) and citric acid. Mix a ratio of 4:1 (4 parts potassium citrate to 1 part citric acid) solution. Both of these ingredients are available at pharmacies and most grocery stores. This acts to reduce the process the plant goes through in response to the injury and slows or hopefully stops the browning. This is another step that takes time but if it is the only way to get a good initiation it is worth trying. After cutting and soaking for as long as one hour in the .125 percent Vitamin C solution continue with your sterilization process for your explant. To make a .125 percent solution add 1.25 grams of Vitamin C to a liter of water.

The most that can be done is cut your oversized explant under a Vitamin C solution, sterilize your oversize explant, and rinse in sterile water. Next trim the cut ends shorter and plate it onto media with Vitamin C and activated charcoal. Keep in a low light space with less than 5mg/L of BAP in the media. Try it with more than 5 initiation vessels before giving up or moving on.

Understanding MicroMols

Micro-mols is a topic that is often misunderstood. The term is often seen and immediately turns potential tissue culturists away because of the difficulty in which it is used. Most often a protocol will state X amount μM or μMol of a plant growth regulator. Figuring out how many mg per ml can be difficult or impossible to figure out on your own.

Plant growth regulators have different molecular weights. Researchers often publish their findings in terms of mg/l instead of micromolar. This is acceptable if only one plant growth regulator is being tested. When using multiple plant growth regulators the best way to compare them is to use micromoles because it conveys quantity by weight, not solution.

For example, 1 mg of BAP and 1 mg of NAA do not have the same number of molecules and there will be more molecules of NAA available to the plant than BAP. This is similar to the pound of bricks and a pound of feathers example. Scientific papers use this method to keep track of comparison available to plant cells. It is quite valuable and useful information but must be converted from µM or µMole to mg/ml for ease of use.

To do this find the molecular weight of the plant growth regulator. Let's use for example 20 uM BAP per liter of media. To find how many milligrams of BAP equals 20uM take the molecular weight of 1uM of BAP (2253 g/l) and multiply that by how many uM we need. First, move the decimal place over 3 spaces to the left which gives .2253 mg.

.2253 mg multiplied by 20 uM gives us 4.506 mg of BAP. Rounding up or down very slightly is often acceptable and makes measurement easier. Add 4.5 mg of BAP to a liter of media. 20uM BAP/l is 4.5 mg/l to replicate the protocol paper requirements for the plant growth regulator.

Occasionally a protocol calls for a quantity of plant growth regulators with a superscript number behind it such as $10^{(-7)}$ M of BAP. The (-7) in your formula means you will be moving the decimal place to the left seven places. There are a couple of steps to get the amount in mg/l to make media.

BAP has a molecular weight of 225.3 g. Moving the decimal over 7 spaces to the left would give 0.00002253 mol. Multiply this number by 10 since the formula calls for "10" units (-7). This moves the decimal point over one space to the right and that value is .00002253.

Change the number into micromol (a millionth of a mol, 1,000,000 th) by moving the decimal point to the right six places. This shows 22.53 µM of BAP. This shows there are 0.2253 milligrams for every 1 µM of BAP so multiply 22.53 µM by 0.2253 mg and it shows 5.076009 milligrams is equal to 22.53 µM. It is okay to round this to 5 mg and it shows the protocol calls for 5mg/l of BAP.

Many protocols list amounts of PGRs to use in micro mols. Some math is required to find the proper amount to use. It isn't terribly difficult to understand how to find the proper amounts to use to make media. Photo by Edward Johnson

These methods of comparison don't seem to be a very easy way to record how much of a plant growth regulator is needed but this is how they are written in many scientific papers.

Fortunately, this is the most dedicated math skills need to be for tissue culture. The metric system itself is pretty easy to navigate around and the most difficulty will be dealing with these µM measurements. Once micro mols are understood this part is much easier.

There will be a few uses for 1 micro mol solutions (1 µM solution) and making a 1 µM solution is simple. The molecular weight of any substance dissolved in 1,000 ml of water makes for a 1 µM solution.

If there is a need to make a 1 μM solution of BAP simply use the molecular weight of BAP, which is 225.3mg (that is 1 μM BAP) dissolved in a liter of water. It is a 1 μM BAP solution.

Tackle just about any protocol that can be found that calls for μM or measurements like 10(-7). This is one of the hardest topics with plant tissue culture to figure out.

Making 1MG/ML Solutions

Liquid solutions can be prepared ahead of time. When needed to make a few vessels quickly, or a lot of vessels even faster, having everything ready is a time and headache saver. Plant growth regulators that have been prepared in a solution with 1 milligram per 1 milliliter will make it very easy to use.

When prepared in a 1 milligram per 1 milliliter solution 'X' amount of chemical is measured out. If media protocol calls for 5mg/l of BAP all that is needed to do is measure out 5ml of the prepared solution and put it into the media. Weighing out 5 milligrams of dry powdered chemical each time would be time-consuming. Not all hormones and chemicals are water-soluble and each time would need extra work to weigh, measure, and dissolve it.

Measuring a solution that has 1 milligram of a chemical with 1 milliliter of liquid makes measuring very simple. Most protocols call for X milligrams per liter. With 1mg/ml solutions and the protocol needs 5mg/l take 5 milliliters into a pipette from the solution bottle and be assured that there are 5 milligrams of the chemical there.

100ml jars of chemicals may not always be convenient but as an example use 100 ml as a standard example for ease of explanation. To make more or less simply adjust the volume proportionally. 50ml is easy to make by cutting the measurements of ingredients by 50 percent and it still creates a 1mg/ml solution.

Measure on the scale 100 mg of dry chemical to be used. BAP is a common plant growth regulator used so here is BAP as an example. Weigh 100 mg of BAP and place it into a small plastic condiment cup. Add a few drops of 91 percent rubbing alcohol and mix until it is completely dissolved. Use a few drops at a time until it is thoroughly dissolved into a liquid. Use as little alcohol as possible to dissolve the BAP but dissolve it completely.

Using a graduated 100ml container add 100mg of dissolved BAP into the graduated container. Fill the container the rest of the way up with RO or distilled water to reach the 100ml level. RO and distilled water have little dissolved solids and allow more solids to be dissolved. There is now 100 milliliters of liquid with 100 mg of BAP contained and dissolved within. 1mg/ml is now the concentration of BAP and using it is as easy as drawing out the amount in milliliters needed in milligrams. Store in the refrigerator or freezer.

Other plant growth regulators that are not water or alcohol soluble need to be diluted with a stronger agent. Most of these other plant growth regulators can be dissolved using a 1 µM solution of sodium hydroxide.

Sodium hydroxide (NaOH) is a highly corrosive and potentially dangerous acid that must be handled safely while wearing eye protection and gloves. Do not get it on your skin or eyes.

Do not add water to sodium hydroxide (NaOH) directly as a fire could result. Add sodium hydroxide to the water slowly so that it does not produce too much heat too quickly.

Store sodium hydroxide (NaOH) in a dark and dry tightly sealed container that is clearly labeled. Add sodium hydroxide (NaOH) slowly to water as it can create a great amount of heat and potentially break a glass measuring container. Breaking a container with NaOH can result in burned skin and other serious injuries or fire.

Do not be careless working with NaOH!

To make a solution that can be used to dissolve these other plant growth regulators make a 1 µM (micro mol) solution of NaOH also known as sodium hydroxide (which is explained in the MicroMols chapter). For sodium hydroxide, the molar weight is 39.997 g/mol, add its molecular weight of 39.997 grams to 1 liter of Reverse Osmosis (RO) or distilled water.

Slowly add the powder to about 750 ml of water. After adding the NaOH powder fill the container the rest of the way up to the 1000ml volume with RO or distilled water.

It is not advisable to make a liter of this solution and for realistic use, 100ml would be better as it should be further diluted to more safely use it to dissolve plant growth regulators.

1 µM NaOH Solution		
Concentration	**NaOH Amount**	**Water**
1 µM NaOH	39.97 grams	1 Liter Water
0.1 µM NaOH	3.99 grams	1 Liter Water
100 ml 0.1 µM	.399 grams	100 ml Water

Potassium hydroxide (KOH) can also be used to dissolve plant growth regulators. It too is a very caustic and dangerous chemical if care and precautions are not used.

To make a 1 M solution of KOH use its molar weight of 56.11 m/mol. Adding 56.11 grams to 1 liter of water will give a 1 µM solution of KOH.

This is also another solution that doesn't need a full liter of. Making 100ml of this solution would be a better option. Dilute this further to use for dissolving plant growth regulators by adding 100ml of the KOH solution to 900ml of distilled or RO water to make a 0.1 µM solution to more safely dissolve powders. It is safer to dissolve hormones in this diluted solution of 0.1 µM KOH. Add 5.6 grams of KOH to one liter of water.

Using the more dilute solution also results in less pH differences when adding the hormone solution to your media, making it easier to get the media pH to the 5.6 to 5.8 pH range.

To make a 1mg/ml solution with a plant growth regulator dissolve the appropriate weight of powder in half of the final solution volume using a 0.1M KOH solution. Carefully stir in the powder gently until it has dissolved. Fill to the final volume. For example: to make a 100ml bottle of 1mg/ml BAP measure out 100mg of BAP. Place the BAP into the beaker and slowly add 50 or 60 ml of 0.1M KOH into the beaker. Gently and carefully stir until dissolved. Once mostly dissolved top off the volume in the beaker to 100ml. There is now a 100ml beaker of 1mg/ml of BAP.

In small volumes, it's best to dissolve the plant growth regulator first with a small amount of solvent and add it to a partial amount of distilled water (not the full amount of your final volume, say

100ml, or there will be more than 100ml solution for instance) and then bring up the total amount of stock solution by adding more distilled water to the graduated measuring container to reach the final volume.

1 µM KOH Solution		
Concentration	**KOH Amount**	**Water**
1 µM KOH	56.11 grams	1 Liter Water
0.1 µM NaOH	5.6 grams	1 Liter Water
100 ml .1 µM	.56 grams	100ml Water

Some basic measurements must be properly calculated to the proper concentration. It isn't overly difficult but caution is needed to ensure that your calculations and measurements are done properly. Photo by Edward Johnson

NaDCC Sterilizer

NaDCC is Sodium dichloroisocyanurate and commonly available at hardware and department stores as a pool chemical for sanitizing swimming pools. NaDCC is a very effective and affordable way to sterilize explants for the tissue culture lab.

It is at least as effective for sterilization as a combination of Mercuric Chloride and Calcium hypochlorite, and it's much milder and safer.

Mix solutions in smaller batches to use before they age too long and possibly lose some of their effectiveness. In dry powder form, it is very stable and will last a long time if kept safely closed and dry.

NaDCC has a lower pH (around 6.8 pH) in solution than regular bleach making this a more effective disinfectant for the same amount of chlorine. A pH closer to 5.8 is preferable as the media protocol for most plants requires a 5.8 pH in the final media. This pH level is more desirable because plants uptake nutrients much better at 5.8 pH.

Phytotoxicity is usually low when using lower concentrations of Na-DCC. 500 PPM (Parts Per Million) solution makes a good explant cleaner and is more gentle than bleach solutions or alcohol. The best benefit from NaDCC is that a lower PPM (Parts Per Million) can be used for an extended sterilization time for heavily infected plant material.

Since it is more gentle on plant tissue, the plant material can be left in longer with the benefit of killing off more contaminants yet maintaining plant health.

For disinfecting delicate plants like the traps from Venus flytraps and the pitchers from sarracenia a lower PPM (Parts Per Million) of chlorine around 250 to 500 would be good. Rinse the explants first in running tap water and place them in a tube with enough NaDCC solution to cover them generously.

Add a drop of baby shampoo to act as a surfactant to get down to the plant's surface and let them soak for as long as an hour or more as part of the sterilization process.

Older material that has been exposed to the outside may have a lot of contaminants on them. Hardwood cuttings, when trying to use buds, might be a good example of when to use higher concentrations. For these applications try a concentration as high as 5000 PPM (Parts Per Million).

Many plants don't have available sterilization protocols, especially for NaDCC, so some experimentation needs to be done regarding whether they will tolerate a 24-hour soak in NaDCC. It is very well worth trying on delicate and hard to sterilize material in various lengths of time.

NaDCC can be used to sterlize explant material as well as your hood and work tools. Pool cleaner is available in differing concentrations. With some calculations the proper concentration solution can be made. Photo by Edward Johnson

250 ppm is good for a 24-hour soak which is better for more delicate explants or more contaminated material. Shorter times will also work well on lightly infested samples or very delicate plants.

At 5000 ppm (Parts Per Million) it would be used for up to an hour with heavily contaminated hardwood cuttings.

After deciding whether you need a high or low concentration for your explant material you must mix the NaDCC to a specific PPM (parts per million) that you plan on using.

The first step is finding the powder form of the product concentration. Look at the package and find what the percentage of chlorine is for the pool cleaner being used. Use that number on your package to calculate the concentration.

A few drops placed on the surface of the medium at a concentration of about 25 ppm can help prohibit contaminants from growing in your vessels. This can be done when initially inoculating the vessel with the explant material or if contamination grows in a vessel. It is worth trying before throwing the vessel out if it isn't badly contaminated so check your vessels regularly.

Autoclaving NaDCC in the media will heat the chlorine and it will off-gas out of solution. This is why it must be placed in the vessel after autoclaving.

One great technique for trying to get a sterile explant is a quick dip in alcohol, then a direct quick dip in 10 or 20 percent bleach solution. After that, the material for the explant is moved to a 400 or 500 PPM solution and is not rinsed further.

Many plants have shown great results without rinsing in sterile water. This saves another step and makes culturing faster. It is a tool to consider to experiment with as time and effort saved can mean fewer contaminated vessels if done properly and successfully. Some very delicate plants will however need to be rinsed in sterile water for success.

NaDCC is not an end-all cure-all solution to sterilizing explant material but it has its merits and uses. It is easy to find and it is easy to work with. The powder mixes easily and stores easily as does the liquid solution. NaDCC is a valuable tool for those practicing plant tissue culture.

There are two ways to find the PPM (Parts Per Million) of NaDCC for making solutions. Use both of these to check against each other to verify the correct amount if preferred.

Method one is the easiest. Find the available chlorine percentage on the pool cleaner label of NaDCC. Find the ratio of pool cleaner to the amount of available chlorine. It is usually clearly stated on the back label.

An example packet of pool cleaner is 63% NaDCC and 39% available chlorine. We will divide 100 percent by the amount of available chlorine [100/39= 2.56410256].

This means that it takes 2.5641 times the amount of pool cleaner to get a certain PPM (Parts Per Million) amount of available chlorine. 1 mg of available chlorine per liter will give a 1 PPM (Part Per Million) solution. Now find the weight amount of the pool cleaner needed by multiplying the PPM (Part Per Million) of chlorine needed by this number 2.5641.

To get a 500 PPM (Parts Per Million) of NaDCC. 500 PPM would equal 500mg multiplied by 2.5641 equals 1282.05 mg or 1.282 grams of NaDCC pool cleaner to make a 500 PPM solution.

Another way to find PPM (Parts Per Million) using NaDCC pool cleaner is to look at the percent of available chlorine on the package. One brand has 56 percent available chlorine. Some kind of standard is needed to be achieved so use .05 percent solution which will make it easier to adjust for various strengths by adjusting the amount of water used.

With 56 percent available chlorine make a .05 percent solution. [.05 divided by 56] = [.00089286] and multiply this by 1000. This gives .89285714 which can be rounded to 893 milligrams per liter of water after moving the decimal point over to get milligrams.

Further examples of this same product would be as follows.

25 PPM solution needs 44.65 mg/L of NaDCC
100 PPM solution needs 178.6 mg/L of NaDCC
250 PPM solution needs 446.5 mg/L of NaDCC
500 PPM solution needs 893 mg/L of NaDCC
1000 PPM solution needs 1.786 g/L of NaDCC

These are only examples. Each product will have its own availability that must be used making calculations for proper concentrations.

Bleach in Tissue Culture

Bleach is an invaluable tool used in plant tissue culture. It can be used to sterilize your explants, tools, and your workstation. Bleach is easy to find at nearly any market. Most household bleach is labeled with the percentage of sodium hypochlorite, buy 5.25% sodium hypochlorite.

Some brands have 8.25% sodium hypochlorite so unless you want to adjust your measurements and calculations avoid this as well. Do not buy bleach that is not labeled with the percentage of sodium hypochlorite. Do not buy bleach with additives such as scents or colors.

Bleach is normally in a concentration of 10 to 20 percent. Normally there is no need to be concerned about getting parts per million or other percentages. The easiest way to obtain a 10 or 20 percent solution is to measure in a 1 liter graduated vessel. For a 10 percent solution of bleach add 100ml of bleach and 900ml of tap water. For a 20 percent solution simply pour 200ml of bleach and 800ml of tap water into the container.

The metric system makes it easy for us to make smaller batches. To make 100ml of a 10 percent bleach solution pour 10ml of bleach and 90ml of water. Subsequently, to make a 20 percent solution of bleach we would add 20ml of bleach and 80ml of tap water.

To make a 500 PPM (Part Per Million) solution of bleach using 5.25% sodium hypochlorite add 9.52ml of bleach and fill to 1-liter volume with water.

A ten percent bleach solution (1 part bleach to 9 parts water) with normal levels of household bleach will yield a 5000 to 6000 PPM solution of available chlorine.

For sterilizing clean tools bleach can be used in a 10 percent or 1/10th bleach solution. Dip the tools in the bleach for several seconds and rinse in a 1 percent or 1/100th bleach solution before use. Tools must be clean and free of plant material and gelling agents to sterilize.

Rust or caked-on material on tools and surfaces can harbor areas for spores and bacteria to hide and bleach cannot penetrate quickly enough to kill it. Make sure your tools are wiped clean and free of foreign matter before dipping to ensure sterilization.

Bleach loses its chlorine over time and thereby reduces its efficiency. Bleach is packaged with varying concentrations of sodium hypochlorite by the manufacturer. Newer bottles of bleach would potentially have more chlorine than old outdated bottles. Bleach manufactured in the summer and winter has differing amounts of sodium hypochlorite to account for temperature affected off-gassing.

Overall, this is minimal and there is no need to be of great concern. Make sure the bleach isn't old by looking at the manufacture date on the label.

Bleach is an oxidizer and when it comes into contact with cell walls it breaks them. This results in cell death.

Get tools, explants, and workspace as sterile as possible. Using bleach can make this possible. It can ruin clothing and carpets and it is corrosive to metal tools especially. Work with bleach in a well-ventilated area, avoid mixing it with ammonia and other chemicals. Wash hands and tools after use. Do not get it in the mouth, on the skin, or in the eyes.

Bleach can be used for many tasks in home based plant tissue culture. Cleaning tools and work area is done best with bleach. Hard to sterilize old growth plants also benefit from a bleach dip in varying concentraions. Photo by Edward Johnson

Vinegar and Hydrogen Peroxide

Hydrogen peroxide and vinegar, when mixed, make a gentle but effective decontaminate. It works as an oxidizer attacking cell walls and destroying the cell walls of fungus and bacteria.

Hydrogen peroxide from the pharmacy is usually a 3% solution that will in itself sterilize many delicate seeds. When plain white vinegar is added it becomes stronger. White vinegar has about 5% acetic acid. Both are stable at room temperature, readily available, and mostly safe to store and use without prolonged exposure.

When creating this mixture use a 4 to 1 ratio. Find the amounts of each by the volume of the solution you want to make. If making 500ml divide by 5 and this gives 100ml of white vinegar (5% acetic acid) and 400 ml of hydrogen peroxide (3% hydrogen peroxide).

Heat the vinegar in the microwave for around 1 minute to the point of boiling. This does several things. It helps sterilize the vinegar, accelerate the reaction between the vinegar and hydrogen peroxide, and to destroy any catalytic enzymes or proteins in the vinegar. Pour the room temperature hydrogen peroxide into the vinegar.

Now, this is a stronger oxidizer than chlorine so use the same caution as when using bleach or other strong chemicals. Store the mixture in the refrigerator in a dark bottle. It will lose its effectiveness in a week so only make as much as can be used in a few days.

This mixture can be used by spraying a work surface with a fine mist and draining away excess liquid. Explants can be dipped for extended periods and it also is a good solution to use in sterilizing stubborn explants.

Explant soft tissue can be disinfected with a 1 to 4 min soaking time. Woody and hard plants may benefit from 5 to 10 minutes. Leave hard and woody tissue in long enough to penetrate surface tissue as it is likely more contaminated than soft cuttings.

Sensitive explants may require rinsing before initiation with a sterile water bath but most plants can be initiated without rinsing. This both saves time and reduces residual contamination in the vessel. With hard to get or sensitive plants it is best to use caution and time your first attempts to keep a log on the outcome. In the event the explant is killed refer to notes and reduce the soak time for the next attempt.

Another use of this mixture is that it can be added on top of a contaminated vessel in an attempt to save the culture. Enough can be added, under sterile conditions, to cover newly forming fungus or other contamination. This can lower the pH and can affect the culture and effectiveness of the mixture. Use as little as possible in covering contaminants under the clean hood. It may save an otherwise contaminated and useless culture.

Small amounts of contamiation can sometimes be killed with a vinegar and hydrogen peroxide solution. Pour a thin layer of vinegar and hydrogen peroxide solution into the vessel under your hood. Seal and check on it the next day.
Photo by Edward Johnson

Some success has been had adding several drops to the top of new cultures to create a thin covering for an effect much like Plant Preservative Mixture (PPM), to keep contamination down. Some plants benefit from it and some don't. Experimentation and note-keeping is important when experimenting with these methods. In the long term, they will save time and effort.

Orchid seedlings that have become contaminated can sometimes be saved using this solution. Rinse the contaminated seedlings in distilled water. Wash the seedlings in the 4:1 mixture for 30 seconds to 1 minute. Using sterile distilled water rinse the seedlings three times and replate.

Some plants it works well with but others the pH or oxidation can't handle so some experimentation may be needed to find what is best for a particular plant. Overall it is a very useful tool in your kit for sterilizing explants, tools, and surfaces. It is easy to make and inexpensive. Most importantly it works.

Notes

Glossary

2iP - 6-(y,y-Dimethylallylamino)purine. Plant growth regulator.

2,4D - 2,4-Dichlorophenoxyacetic acid. Plant growth regulator.

Adventitious shoot - Shoots that develop from cells induced or after transplanting. In this context, it describes roots growing from separated rhizomes, tubers, and similar growths.

Autoclave - Machine sterilizing with high heat and high pressure.

Auxin - Plant growth regulator influencing elongation of cells.

BAP - 6-Benzylaminopurine, benzyl adenine, BAP or BA. Plant growth regulator used to induce multiplication mostly.

Benzyl amino purine - Another name for BAP, BA, 6-Benzylaminopurine, or benzyl adenine. They are all the same chemical.

Callus - Undifferentiated cells used to multiply plants and can be influenced to make shoots also.

Cultivar - Typically grown vegetatively as opposed to variety which comes true from seed generally.

Cytokinen - Plant growth regulator that is used generally to induce multiplication of cells and plantlets.

Endemic - Plants that only grow in a geographically small or limited area. They grow nowhere else on earth.

Explant - Donor plant material sterilized for initiation stage.

GA3 - Known as gibberellin A3, GA. Influences cell division and growth. Used for plant multiplication and shoot tip elongation.

Gibberellin - Known also as GA3.

IAA - Indoleacetic acid. Induces root and shoot elongation.

IBA - Indole-3-butyric acid. Auxin and promoting root formation.

Kinetin - Cytokinen that promotes cell division. Used to make callus or shoots. Depends on auxins used.

Meristem - Plant tips that are actively growing fresh new tissue.

Murashige and Skoog - Premade formula of plant growth medium. Very popular for many plants.

NAA - 1-Naphthaleneacetic acid. Auxin used for inducing rooting.

Surfactant - Liquid that lowers the surface tension of a surface.

Zeatin - Cytokinen that induces callus, lateral buds, and cell division for multiplication.

About the Author

Writer, blogger, and hobbyist: he has kept plants and aquariums for more than forty years. His articles have been published in magazines and online.

Propagating plants is one of his favorite pastimes. Aroids and aquatic plants are his favorite. He is always looking to streamline methods of plant propagation.

Edward is also the creator of Biotope One which is home to the Biotope One Plant Library and the Biotope Data Project. The project was set up to help hobbyists grow plants and share them amongst themselves.

He is living in his fourth country over three continents and loves exploring the wilds for new plants and fish.

Made in the USA
Coppell, TX
05 September 2021

61851995R00075